A Journey of Three

The Camino de Santiago

Una Peregrina

ROSE GARDEN BOOKS
Glastonbury, BA6 9JQ, UK

Front cover photograph © Una Peregrina
Used by kind permision

Rear cover map illustration © E. Walker
Used by kind permission

Grateful acknowledgement is made to Frederick Warne Publishers for
permission to reproduce the poems by Cicely Mary Barker
'The Song of The Wayfaring Tree Fairy' on page 49
and 'The Song of The Heather Fairy' on page 340.
Copyright © The Estate of Cicely Mary Barker 1926, 1944.
Reprinted by permission of Penguin Random House.

British Library Cataloguing-in-Publishing Data
A record is available from the British Library
ISBN 978-0-9955103-6-4

CONTENTS

PREFACE

Once upon a time, I walked the Camino de Santiago, the Way, which seems to me to be a River, a river of Life.

I walked in the company of my sons, ten years old then, twins. I cannot imagine more delightful companions, nor wiser teachers, than that splendid duo; they were curious, always in-the-moment, eager to explore and discover, profoundly trusting, of me, of the Way, of Santiago. They were so courageous, so full of laughter, so kind, so free. We stopped to investigate all that caught their attention, and the Way miraculously shaped time to those pauses, those insights, that vibrant attention.

The Camino has been alive in me from my childhood, presenting itself in countless nudges, from scallop shells to dreams, which I can look back on and recognize now as the Camino calling me, but it took a long time to hear, and longer still to answer.

Over time, the yearning to walk became a compulsion. To be compelled is to be humbled before the Divine. It became absolutely clear that my sons must also go, that this journey was for the three of us. We committed to a window of time and travelled with the support and prayers of our village, among them, dear C, J, M, B, D, K, A, G, L, S, V and N.

We began our Camino with excitement and trepidation. Again and again, we three were told that the boys were the first to walk from Saint-Jean-Pied-de-Port in generations. From village to village, the grapevine sent word ahead, and the elders would be watching for them. Again and again, we were met from a place of sacredness, respect, gratitude, and love. We felt that deeply. The beauty of those many gestures perfumed our way.

We walked for peace, for the world's peace, in the name of peace, singing the song of peace, contemplating peace, praying for Peace Love Peace Love. The prayers for peace that we sent out echoed and added to the millions of others sent from hearts and minds across the planet that year.

At the wonderful Pilgrims Office in Saint-Jean-Pied-de-Port, we were advised to speak and think positively along the Camino. Such a blessing, that advice!

We learned to say hello to everyone. *Hola* or *buenos dias* or *buen dia*. We were respectful. It was new for everyone to have children staying in the refugios and albergues. People were mostly kind to us. Mostly considerate of one another. Mostly. Sad to say, we also witnessed ugly Americans and ugly Canadians and ugly Germans.

We were constantly aware of, and grateful for, the villagers and folk along the way. Every day more and more people walk through their villages. A relentless torrent now. For so many walkers, the Camino is not a religious or spiritual pilgrimage, rather, it is a number of kilometres to be conquered.

And yet, and yet, the Camino works upon the soul, will ye or nil ye.

We learned to be gentle with all walkers, to think of all as pilgrims, even the very abrasive ones. We learned to listen to the inner "still small voice". Oh we learned, with every step we took.

Now, years on, I have become able to approach the mystery and miracles of our journey. Now and always, I send profound thanks to the hospitaleros, those kind folk of refugios and albergues, and, to each and everyone who helped us on our Way.

Out of respect for the anonymity of pilgrims (ourselves and others) and the anonymity of the kind hospitaleros, and the anonymity of the dear people who live along the Camino, and those sweet folk in our village – *to honour the sacredness of our journeys all* – I have used just a symbolic letter as an indicator, rather than actual names.

Thus, the pilgrimage itself, the Way, comes into focus.

I offer all to you with the hope that,
in walking with us every day,
you too will be blessed by the Camino,
you too will come to Santiago transformed.

Breathe
A White Rose
In and Out
See the petals move as you breathe
Feel the space within you expand...

PARIS

We begin in Paris, the City of Light, a beginning point of the pilgrimage route to Santiago de Compostela since medieval times. Our quiet old-fashioned hotel is in the $5^{\text{ième}}$, near Les Gobelins tapestry factory. The boys' bedspread has scallop shells on it! How perfect! In the morning, after café au lait (with scallop shells on the sugar tongs!) and hot chocolate and jus d'orange and baguettes with butter and jam, we board a city bus, the 47, to Notre-Dame Cathedral, T and M staring out the windows. A shop that sells chess sets catches their attention. There is so much to see, so many shops, so many people! We disembark and take turns standing at Point Zero, the disc in the ground in front of Notre-Dame.

Outside, thence inside. Scallop shells on the water basin make me smile and nod. I have been here so many times, over so many decades, and have not paid conscious attention to this before. One of our favourite statues of Mary is here, venerated. Above and around her, the exquisite light refracts through stained glass and time. I send a loving thought to our dear friends, recently married here. Next, we purchase a few souvenirs, knowing they are intended as gifts for people we have yet to meet on the Camino, the Way, the Ray of Light. We return outside, and this time, sight ourselves along the Way with our feet on Point Zero .. across the Seine .. along the rue Saint-Jacques. This is a beginning, I feel it in my bones. (dot dot .. left, right .. left, right .. the cadence of walking ..)

Crossing the Seine, our first pause is in the courtyard of the Musée de Cluny, with its sundial and scallop shells. We continue walking along the rue Saint-Jacques. The boys are finding the city interesting, but not enlivening, compared to their idea of the Camino, so I suggest a detour to a pâtisserie, and then I surprise them and we go into the Jardin de Luxembourg and they sail the famous model sailboats, happily happily immersed in wind and water, dashing around the little lake. Bright sails, bright smiles.

We return to the rue Saint-Jacques and continue, spotting a plaque for the Chemin de St Jacques (the Way of St James, el Camino de Santiago) at the church of Saint-Jacques du Haut-Pas. A while later, Le Val-de-Grâce appears. We must go in. This is the church that Anne of Austria built. She had prayed for a son, and promised a church in return. That son grew up to become Louis XIV. Looking at the opulence of this church, one sees that childhood imprint on his every gesture. Anne chose this site because it was on the pilgrimage route to Santiago de Compostela. The land was then in the countryside rather than completely embraced by Paris as it is now. The convent, which she also built in gratitude, became renowned as a place of respite and healing for pilgrims. The vale of Grace. Of course. At the end of our day, I am aware that we have walked through centuries today, not mere kilometres.

Today is your day!
You're off to Great Places!
You're off and away!..

Dr. Seuss

Oh, The Places You'll Go!

Paris to Saint-Jean-Pied-de-Port

6:30 and we are up and out. The boys are so fabulous! Across to the 91 bus stop just as it pulls up. Early Saturday morning. Quiet. Market setting up. Off at Gare Montparnasse. An LED sign warns against pickpockets. The boys have a great technique for standing guard at cashpoints, flanking me, facing out. We are always safe. Breakfast at the train station café – step up to the bar and one of five fellows gets your order, in oh, 30 seconds. Done! Change in the dish (not in the hand). Scrumptious croissants and perfectly decent machine coffee. Finally our TGV comes up on the board and we head toward it, M and T telling me how they hope to meet kind, happy children on the train. The TGV is the length of two normal trains, so we walk hurriedly past carriage after carriage. We find ours and begin to settle in, only to be displaced by a man, his daughter and her dog, because we are somehow in the wrong carriage. So, we move along and finally locate our compartment, which has four seats and a table with a window between it and the corridor, where there are two other seats facing one another. Lo and behold, our fourth is a sweet-faced girl of seven whose brother (age ten) and mother are sitting in the couloir (corridor) seats! This is the right car .. and so begins six hours of delightfulness! The maman and I sit in the couloir seats, and the children play in the compartment. We speak of many things, she speaking English, I, French. She sees our backpacks and wants to know if we are Christian (she is), and if we understand that it is a religious journey, this pilgrimage, and that it is to be taken seriously. I respectfully concur. The backdrop for our conversation is gorgeous countryside with beautiful châteaux, which I see reflected in the glass behind O's head as she chatters away. The boys are already hearing the music of the language, understanding phrases as they laugh and play games with R and H. The delightful trio descend at Dax, off to their country home. We continue to Bayonne. Here, the landscape is harsh somehow. O had said it was a desert, with quicksand, here in the Middle Ages. This, from a book she is reading, *Les Reines de France*. I think of the pilgrims journeying then, imagining a fraught desert landscape. We arrive in the small station at Bayonne, to change to our train to Saint-Jean.

It turns out to be a tiny, one-carriage, rather weatherbeaten "train". A slow slow hot whistle-blowing journey, in and out of tunnels, waving to onlookers. I point out to the boys that this slowness is perfect, as we ratchet down from aeroplane to TGV to this. There are nine other pilgrims in this little carriage with us, and one dog. The boys are processing all of this whilst reading. M has six books of a delightful series in his backpack. This, in addition to his copy of Marcus Aurelius' *Meditations* and his journal. T has his journal and his copy of *Zen Flesh, Zen Bones*. The Journey becomes more real, a bit more gritty and dusty, everyone's eyes contemplative. It is a huge thing here in France, this pilgrimage route. We are so blessed to be able to do this; am feeling a bit teary with gratitude.

Arriving in Saint-Jean, we clamber down onto a tiny wooden box, and then the ground, adjusting our packs, as a small crowd tries to leap on. Oh look at the town! It's charming! Sunny! Birds singing. Just around the corner from the teeny tiny train station is a shop with ice cream. Delicious! Two happy boys and I amble around the bend and up across the busy street into the heart of Saint-Jean-Pied-de-Port. We come to the Pilgrims Office but I cannot stop yet, must find our auberge. Up and up, the scale of this tiny cobblestone street is impeccable!

Through the citadel gate, then, there on the left, our auberge, in a house built in 1637. H, the English owner, is most welcoming. Once settled, we return to the Pilgrims' Office and fill out our paperwork and get our first stamps in our *credenciales* and learn about pack weight (we are chastised, told ours are too heavy) and about the Camino. We are told with deep solemnity to always use words in a positive way on the Camino. It is a route of miracles! After listening for a bit, M and T politely ask to leave so they can climb to the castle/citadel. They dash off, and I learn about Santiago and the Way from the volunteer, so lovely. Her kindness fills my heart. *"Vous demandez et Saint Jacques vous le donnez!"* Together again, the boys and I thoroughly explore the town, falling in love with one shop that sells absolutely every interesting thing a pilgrim might want. You see, sometimes people come to Saint-Jean and are suddenly compelled to walk, and this shop has everything everything.

We have dinner at a bistro. They give us a little plate of paté on bread, it tastes so restorative! And when I step to the bar to pay, the man tells me it is a gift, and I know it is really a blessing. Later that evening, H tells us stories about the Way, and gives us each a scallop shell, the symbol of the pilgrim of the Camino de Santiago, to wear on our packs. (O Paris, your scallop shells, your mementos .. my pilgrim's purse from Sainte-Chapelle last September ..) And here again, a shell. A blessing, this journey of generosity .. *Thank you Santiago!*

I walk with
My staff of hope/support/protection
My pouch of faith/sustenance
My shell of light/god/love

SAINT-JEAN-PIED-DE-PORT TO ORISSON

The first sound is the strum of a harp, my alarm. The second, as if in answer, is a bird warbling the loveliest song in our first moments awake. Breakfast includes award-winning sheep's milk cheese and heavenly local chorizo and jambon, and amazing bread, and blueberry jam "from just nearby". H thinks that the huge upsurge in pilgrims started with a book a German man wrote some fifteen years ago about the Pays Basque. He says about the Basque people, "No one knows where they came from, nor their language, but they've been here some 3,000 years." He offers a Basque joke: "The Romans came and the Basques said hello. The Romans left and the Basques said good bye," and laughs uproariously.

We treasure this lovely leisurely morning .. the boys have me email their dad asking for the latest issue of Popular Science which has an article on new flying machines .. such a happy range of conversation. It's 9:20 when we finally head out, with our lunch of hardboiled eggs and cheese and chorizo in a tidy package. We leave the boys' jeans as a *donativo* with the lovely lady of the Pilgrims Office. Full of excitement, our packs adjusted, we walk down the quiet Sunday morning street to the beautiful fountain.

We start to fill our water bottles, then stop, listening. The hallelujahs emanating from the church cause us to step in .. and we are in time for the last of the beautiful service. Then out to fill our bottles. We step into the church again for a quick nod of prayer, returned, with a smile, from the priest. Outside is the lovely kind woman from the Pilgrims' Office, alone on the street, waiting for us! She tells us she feels we will have good luck. Then with a smile and a *"Bonne chance!"* she waves us onward, my heart murmuring its gratitude.

Up and out in glorious sun. 100 metres up the hill, we shed our outer layers. Such a beautiful walk! (dot dot, left, right ..) The first six kilometres are replete with whitewashed farmhouses with deep red shutters, pots of violets, fields of sheep (not Irish darlings, but if these are the cheese makers, thank you!) .. sunshine touching all, expansive views .. my gaze directed up and up. Other pilgrims and day hikers pausing for a moment to chat with us. The locals have long wooden walking sticks, and the pilgrims, shorter wooden sticks or metal collapsible poles, or none. One fellow has walked here from Brittany! Another has cycled the whole route and is now walking. He says *"Bon courage"* to the boys, as does most everyone. As the path narrows between rocks, we come upon a baby vole (or mole, we aren't sure which, the long nose, the funny feet). It is so precious and small and panting with fear at being caught in the open. The boys make a little haven for it off the path, complete with soft sheep's wool they have pulled off the fencing. They talk to the little darling, soothing it, then carefully move it without touching it, so it won't smell like humans to its mother or father. It seems so reassured in its haven, looking at them with its bright eyes. Smiles all around. We pause for a moment of offerings to the fairy folk, to the plants and animals of this beautiful valley. It is good.

We climb higher and higher. The boys' packs are so heavy (12 and 13 kg) so we stop and do stretches. We climb, with our stuff, metaphors heavy in my mind, (and remembered admonishments - no more than 10% packweight, especially for children, said the volunteer in the Pilgrim's Office). We walk and pause and think and chatter and gaze at the beauty around us and listen to the birds singing, "reach for the sky!" A favourite prayer comes to mind ..

In a sacred manner I am walking.
With visible tracks I am walking.
In a sacred manner I walk.

Thus I feel the companionship of White Buffalo Woman. The sun bathing all in golden light, the village in miniature below us now.

We leave the paved road and climb, the ground and rocks markedly more comfortable. We stop at a water source with its pump. M offers me some from his drinking shell (the one from the Pilgrims Office, different from the one from H, which is attached to his pack). We are so high that, as was said in the *Liber Sancti Jacobi* (12th century), "Those who climb up here think they are touching the sky." As we get closer and closer to the deep blue sky, T holds out his scallop shell and says, laughing, "Skywater, fill my cup." Santiago obliges. Within a few seconds the skies are dark grey and it is pouring rain!! His shell is filled in less than one breath. We grab our pack covers and raingear, even though we are soaked, then duck our heads and face into the rain, curving around the mountaintop.

I am vividly remembering the woman yesterday in the Pilgrims Office who told me to pay close attention to what was asked for, because Santiago hears all. At the Auberge Orisson, they take pity on the drenched boys so they turn on the heat in our room! The bear cubs are tumbling and laughing on their bed. *Thank you Santiago!*

First: Things can never touch the soul,
but stand inert outside it,
so that disquiet can arise
only from fancies within.

Second: All visible objects change
in a moment
and will be no more.. the whole universe is change
and life itself is but what you deem it.

Marcus Aurelius

Meditations IV.3

ORISSON TO RONCESVALLES

We start our day with bowls of steaming hot chocolate and café au lait, and with many thanks to the proprietor, *"Merci pour la chauffage!"* Amidst many kind farewells of *"Buen camino"* and *"Bon chemin"*, we step out .. into the clouds! There is a moment where we leave the tarmac for the waymarked trail .. that must symbolize something, the "road less travelled" perhaps. Higher and higher, colder and colder, no visibility, exhausted and a bit frightened, we ask the fairies for help. We think we have walked eight kilometres, so we are hopeful and cold and exhausted, peering through the mist for the mountain hut where we might rest and recover a bit .. but somewhere we must have missed the sign for it, and I realize, with a sick feeling, that we can neither turn back in our disorientation, nor stop because we do not know if the weather will worsen. So we continue walking carefully, each of us doing our best to keep a stiff upper lip .. We do not ever see more than a couple of metres in front of us, our bright orange backpack covers barely visible.

In a total whiteout somewhere, I slip and slide downhill, catching myself on a rock, and the boys pull me back up with the climbing rope that T had insisted upon bringing. I will never know what was below me .. but it felt like air .. and I will never forget the blue of the rope, the texture of it as it touched my fingertips, the boys' voices swirling in the whiteout .. our shared relief, hugging one another. Grateful thanks to the fairy folk, to the Celtic wisdom of Ireland coming through to this Path of the Stars we cannot yet see or feel. We continue to sense our way forward .. suddenly, a brief glimpse of the Camino marker, its yellow bright in the storm .. and then later when we feel certain we are lost, two pilgrims come striding by. *Thank you Santiago!* We follow them for a few minutes until they are gone in the whiteout. This is a pathway of faith, but I did not ever imagine our very lives were entrusted to it. The Way starts to descend, and we come under the clouds a bit, down through a beautiful friendly beech forest, picking our way over slippery boulders and tree roots. We stop in the forest to change wet wool socks for dry ones. I carry the boys' packs for a bit.

When we see the vast wings of the roofline of Roncesvalles monastery, I blurt out, "I've never been so happy to see a building!" I keep my weeping for later, after all, we made it across the

Pyrenees! I am so proud of the boys: 7+ hours nonstop climbing from 700m up to the Col de Loepeder at 1450m (4757 feet), then down to Roncesvalles at 900m .. and this with no more than 2 metres of visibility for kilometre after kilometre of deep snowbanks, or mud. Such a ferocious day. The boys trusting me, and me? Me trusting .. who? Santiago? It has been so hard for me to hold a place of prayer all day, so much fear, so much pain, so strange to walk and walk blindly.

We are so relieved to come to the Pilgrim's office at the refugio, to gratefully wait the twenty minutes to get checked in. M and T discuss inventions they have in mind. The Dutch volunteers help us get settled in. We pay to have our muddy clothes washed. They insist, and it feels so kind that my earlier unshed tears come flooding out. Now, hot showers. Our boots are full of newspapers so that they will be dry for tomorrow's walking.

The refugio is a huge, centuries-old stone building, built in 1130, shaped like the nave of a church, built to house pilgrims. 120 of us are sleeping here tonight, in this one vast space. The boys are the only children here. One of the volunteers takes us to where the tour of the monastery buildings starts. We see Charlemagne's chess set, a famous emerald, an ossuary where the boys see their first skulls and longbones. History, swirling and landing like ravens.

We are next directed to last-minute tickets for dinner, and are so grateful because it is delicious! Hot veg soup followed by whole roasted trout. M separates meat from bones with his most scientific mien. A Frenchman next to us is so impressed with the boys, with their freedom of expression, with their willingness to ask questions, that he tells them emphatically and urgently, in French: *your freedom is so important .. others will try to influence you but try not to be influenced .. keep your freedom!* The end of the day is the Pilgrims Mass and Blessing. I look at the faces and posture of all of these people, all reaching for something that the Camino will, hopefully, answer. The blessing seems to settle over each of us as a mantle.

We return to the now-full refugio. Our laundry is done, such a gift! The classical music being played wafts people into a different time. I give foot massages to the boys, sending them to a restorative sleep. It is lovely to feel so safe and cared for after the walk today .. which so often felt only precarious. I have an amazing conversation with another Frenchman about Finisterre .. the end of the earth .. what lies beyond .. the unknown .. mystery .. the Grace of the Divine .. the ocean ..

the vastness of all that is. It seems to me to be some sort of contemplative prayer, this conversation .. one of recognition, of affirmation, so different from my pleading for help and sustenance earlier. I learn a wonderful Dutch word, *uitwaaien*, which the volunteers tell me means 'out walking in windy weather for fun'. This is a sustaining word. *Good night Santiago (and Co.), and thank you!*

I rise today
Through
Strength of heaven
Light of sun
Radiance of moon
Splendor of fire
Speed of lightning
Swiftness of wind
Depth of sea
Stability of earth
Firmness of rock

Celtic prayer

Roncesvalles to Espinal

I hear the music first, familiar, classical, then realize the lights are on. 6am. The night-time rustles and creaks and rummages and footsteps, and snoring, are at an end. I lie still and listen to the room wake up .. sound building upon sound until it is a wave rushing through this huge space.

M in his top bunk awakened at 6:30. He is writing in his journal. I stretch and listen and watch the flow of pilgrims. By 7, when T awakens, most have gone out and onward. All must be gone by 8, and so are we, after the volunteer wishes us *Buen camino* and tells us that Burguete (and a bakery!) are just 2 kilometres away. We set off in the direction he points out. Then into the woods, a wide pleasant path, well-marked. Each time we feel we need confirmation that we are on the Way, the scallop shell and arrow appear. One time it makes me laugh, as the time from my beginning fear and the appearance of the sign is less than a minute. Begone fear! *Let go and expect goodness.* It turns out that it is 3.2 kilometres to Burguete and that it is as cold and misty as yesterday. Ah well, rather than wait, we stop at the first place we see and find tables full of laughing, talking pilgrims. A coffee, two hot chocolates, five croissants, and such a pleasant time spent reading (the boys have their series, the books even more important to them after having been carried over the Pyrenees) .. and writing. We head out into the cold again.

The next hour is one of the boys happily floating stickboats down a rill along the edge of the empty main street of Burguete. They run up and down, backpacks on, laughing and chattering away. I drift toward the church .. a gorgeous altar, local children singing. I glance toward the boys then step into a little hotel to ask about Hemingway's piano .. it is here somewhere, but they direct me to the opposite end of town. T and M signal that they are ready to continue, so we stride along a lane, observing all delightedly. Shaggy ponies with cowbells on being herded by two men. White old Range Rovers everywhere. A wide lane, flanked by newly planted trees to offer summer shelter in years to come. Rolling farmland and pasture. Cold mist with a biting wind .. it makes me realize that yesterday the wind was at our back, the Irish blessing. Thank you Santiago and St. Patrick! We meet a Korean woman, a pilgrim, whose husband gave her this walk as a present after 27 years of marriage. This is their first time apart in all those

years. Six bridges of huge stone, topped with lintels
.. marvelous to walk over. The water is so clear it
is hard to gauge the depth, which fascinates the
boys. My mind goes again and again to an email
I received this morning .. a vast mystical hopeful
contemplation. As I walk, contemplating, I become
aware of my left foot as love, my right foot as peace,
and .. *Love Peace .. Love Peace .. Love Peace* .. becomes
the metronome, clear and balanced.

Part way up a hill .. yesterday's travails still too
vivid, too weighty, overcome us with exhaustion.
So we agree to stop in Espinal, which will be 6.7
kilometres in total for today. At a slow pace, we
continue, talking about how our attitudes can
affect ourselves and our travelling companions,
for ill or, as strongly, for good. Espinal appears,
and we find we are all equally happy to be stopping
for the day. The sign for a hostel appears and it
feels correct, though a bit off of the Way, but I am
curious, so we walk into the village. Empty. Oddly
disconcerting. So we retrace our steps to the hostel.
Pricey. Clean. Large pleasant room with a balcony.
Great light switches. We collapse a bit. Then I go
foraging and return with scrumptious cheese and
a baguette and Gummy Octopus treats. I feel now,
belatedly, now that we are inside and off the Way
slightly, that we are out of harm's way, that we
have become invisible. Thank you fairy folk. Thank

you Santiago. Perhaps those who pose a danger to us will become caught in an illusion or will be otherwise distracted so that we can travel safely, incognito, and invisibly to them. While the boys contentedly read their books, I meditate, breathing in love, exhaling peace. With each breath I expand the field of loving gentleness around us. Then I read a bit of Paolo Coelho's *The Pilgrimage* aloud which seems to touch on that feeling sense of harm and not harm .. of journey and secret journey .. of explained and unexplained. We venture out for breakfast supplies, and return to the hostel. The boys play with Star Wars story ideas and inventions, their journal pencils standing in for rockets etc. T suddenly, profoundly, says, *"It rests on a pinpoint, everything does. Everything can go toward bad or good from one point."*

We look through a guidebook and can see that we can go from albergue to albergue for the rest of the trip. Tonight, we are three in one room rather than 120. Comparing yesterday with today, we say, as do the Australian aborigines, *"we stop so our souls can catch up with us."*

Last thoughts: *Gods and goddesses, powers that be, thank you for your protection and blessings. Thank you Santiago for watching over us! For this excellent place to rest.*

Nada te turbe,
Nada te espanta.
Todo se pasa,
Solo Dios no se muda..

Let nothing disturb thee,
Let nothing frighten thee.
All things pass..
Only God does not move.

St. Teresa de Avila

Espinal to Zubiri

The alarm does have an inclination to make its
when it's still dark out! Cold mist and wind again.
Uphill and down through stands of beech trees.
Darling small yellow trumpet flowers and some
five petaled flowers in shades of violet, probably
vinca, but I want them to be something Navarran.
I think of the flower fairy poems we love so much,
by Cicely Mary Barker:

The Song of The Wayfaring Tree Fairy

*My shoots are tipped
with buds as dusty-grey
As ancient pilgrims
toiling on their way.
Like Thursday's child
with far to go, I stand
All ready for the road
to Fairyland;
With hood, and bag, and shoes
my name to suit,
And in my hand
my gorgeous-tinted fruit.*

Everyone's journey is so different, including T's and M's and mine; each of us is journeying very differently and yet we are a good team. They are so animated in their discussions, ranging today from physics to books recently read, to endings they would write instead of endings written. I am walking behind them .. sometimes a ways behind them, practising .. *Peace Love .. Peace Love*. This while trying to simultaneously carry another layer of prayer, *May you be at Peace* .. this is directed at everything I see, dirt, rocks, plants, sky, clouds, the boys, the Camino, other pilgrims, the villages, Spain, the world. May you be at Peace. The sun comes out, brightening everything I gaze upon, and finally, long after we cannot bear another step, we come to Zubiri. Beautiful bridge, welcoming river.

We check in at the municipal albergue. It is interesting to me how I become attached to certain people, however briefly. I see this reflected in the faces of people who have passed us during the day, now smiling happily at us as we come into the albergue courtyard. For me today, there was the little old lady, as ancient to me as I am to the boys. T said, "there's a real grandma!" I wanted to offer her some of our cheese and biscuits and I knew she'd be as mad as a hornet. And the German woman just now, aching, looking how we all look when we take our packs and shoes off. I make the mistake of sitting down, rather than dashing to the little store for food before they close for siesta .. so, we are hungry and tired. Oh well, wash our socks, hang them to dry. The store will open later, all will be well. So many people on the Camino today .. many in such a rush. We return to the ancient stone bridge, the river. The boys, in flip flops (heavenly after a day in shoes), are merrily being boys .. can you hear their shouts and the plonks of stones tossed into the river?? I am grateful to be traveling with them. We stop to investigate mud, horses, caterpillars, rocks (such gorgeous rocks today, layers of slate and something that looks like soapstone) .. the Journey is a blessing!

And now here is my secret,
a very simple secret.
It is only with the heart
that one can see rightly.
What is essential
is invisible to the eye.

Antoine de St. Exupéry

Zubiri to Larrasoana

The only way I can keep track of the days is to look back at the day before and add from there. If I did not do that, I would become detached from time .. an idea indeed!

Of course, M is awake first, his alarm is the quiet rustlings of other pilgrims packing. Much to his understandable dismay, we are not out the door until 8am. This is only okay because we have only to walk to Larrasoana. I am tired, and cranky about my sloppily packed backpack, and worried about fatigue. So much fear, too little faith. I try to steer my mind to something positive. We stop within the first few minutes of our walk for breakfast (hot chocolate for the junior set, café con leche for me, plus amazing fresh squeezed orange juice, plus bread with jam and butter), then we begin again, up the hill, and we quickly understand that anything less than a mountain is what is locally termed *plano* (flat)! On the left appears a field full of ponies, tiny shaggy cautious. T drops his pack and dashes for them, then dashes back for his stash of sugar cubes(!) The next hour is spent, well-spent, with the ponies. They are waist high to the boys, with two foals, so tiny, the boys could easily hold them in their arms.

We come upon a laminated card, nailed to a post: *"Wenn du etwas ganz fest willst, dann wird das Universum darauf hinwirken, dass du es erreichen kannst."* I translate for the boys: 'When you really want something, then the entire universe moves to help you achieve it.'

Onward. It is sunny, birds singing their happiness. Long pause for lizard chasing. In contrast to the heat, the many streams burble musically of mountain snows. Butterfly lane: first purple, then orange, then yellow in uncountable flutterings. We wonder who has created the lovely pathways, of granite pieces or flagstone, and the stone bridges across the streams. Treelined lanes adjoining pastures. Mockingbirds. Kites. Sparrow-tailed hawks, their tails shifting 90°, what is the word, aileron? And, what am I doing amidst the beauty? Holding a space for prayer? No, I am fretting about our pace, wondering if we will make it to Santiago de Compostela .. currently we need 62 days but have 58 remaining. T thinks our solution is horses. M wants us to be true pilgrims and walk the entire way. The math of our future days is completely pointless to fret about. Then, feeling tired gets me going about pack weight, my thoughts strident, but I keep them to myself. I realize we packed, before we started on the Camino, from a fear-based place .. what if the sky falls etc etc .. so I fret and walk .. (dot, dot, left, right, peace, love ..) and then what else is there to think about but faith?! Slowly my mind calms, and thus we come into Larrasoana. Medieval. Always welcoming of pilgrims. Beside a river. Peaceful. Tranquil. All is well.

It's such a lovely village, but I am still tired-cranky around the edges. On the heels of yesterday's conversation about attitude impacting others, I am further disappointed with myself for not being a good role model. Ugh. We find a simpatico café and rest in their garden for an hour. We then wait at the albergue for awhile, and I continue waiting while the boys go off to investigate the river. I chat with some of the incoming pilgrims and learn that some pilgrims who started out after us over the Pyrenees did not make it .. lost, and, sadly, probably dead. Shocking. I move away from that news, unclear what to do about it, and join another group. We talk about the value of speaking many languages. Somewhere in the conversation I realize that I am speaking German after twenty something years .. here it is. *Thank you Santiago!*

At check in, they prioritize not per usual, by whose packs are in line, but by favouring a group from Roncesvalles. Then, the boys aren't back as they had said they would be and I start to cry. The hospitalera, elegantly dressed with her pearls, lets me leave our backpacks in the antechamber whilst I run looking. I find them, they are happily happily playing by the river, but I cannot stop crying. I love them so much and could not bear it if anything awful happened to them. I feel the wilderness of this Camino push against me, but I am drowning in my day's accumulated fear and frustration, and the sad news from the Pyrenees, so I cry.

We return to the albergue and the lady tells the boys, in Spanish, that we were all frightened for their safety, and that she and her husband were also looking for them, and that there are many good people on the Camino but also bad people, so they must always be where I can see them, and we must all do as we agree to do, whether to meet at a certain time, etc. It is an intense and upsetting time for all of us. I am so sorry that the boys are in any way chastened, but so wanting them to know how precious they are to me, so I tell them that I must watch over them, differently from how it will be when they are older and bigger. The tears seem to wash things clean, for me anyway, and I apologise to my dear sons who have such generous hearts! So, what else is next, but our laundry! A man, a fellow pilgrim, shows us his technique for drying clothes.

Observations: Everyone smokes. The villages are empty. The bars still are of the Old European way. Pack sizes and weights vary enormously. Quick dry fabric is deemed better than wool, by many pilgrims, except for socks. Swallows dart from nest to sky. So many languages being spoken. Back to laundry. We bring ours, still wet, in to hang from the underside of the upper bunks. People are fascinated by the boys and so pleased we are doing this. They suggest this be a book, a movie, a television series. The boys have recovered their equilibrium. I also. At dinner, an interesting moment, the café owner offers the boys each a soda, regretting earlier not having given them jam when they asked for it. Then the owner keeps trying to feed the boys extra, saying that he wants them to eat a lot and grow big! It becomes a dinner of laughter and conversation in three languages. I am so proud of M and T, already they are hearing the Language of The World. *Thank you Santiago!*

There was an idea in the Middle Ages,
that by going on pilgrimage as Muslim pilgrims do,
you were reinstating the original condition of man.
The act of walking through a wilderness was thought
to bring you closer to God.

Bruce Chatwin

LARRASOANA TO TRINIDAD DE ARRE

At breakfast this morning we share the table with Swiss, French, Swedish, German and Scottish pilgrims. Languages flicker from English to French to German and so it is a happy chattering table. I am used to a certain fluency in French, but am fascinated to find myself having rather involved conversations in German also! Amazing after so little use for so long! Also, the people assume I understand Spanish and so I find myself not only understanding, but translating into German or English or French! Life is full of mystery and gifts! There is a laughter-filled conversation about the sounds animals make in different languages .. and then we are realizing it is highly unlikely we'll see one another again so there is a flurry of hugs and well-wishing. Finally, after a fond farewell to the café owner, the boys and I walk back through the village, not wanting to leave .. and come upon a documentary film crew!

The camera and sound guys bolt from the pilgrim they are talking to and chase after the boys, understandably, for child pilgrims are rare. I keep setting boundaries, over many conversations today, meeting the film crew again and again, asking for our anonymity. The producer finally says she will protect our privacy. I also just about die of jealousy for several hours! My right hip becomes extremely painful. I walk and complain, then T turns to me with a level gaze and asks me if my hip is where I am storing my anger! I am so startled! Yes, and my jealousy too. Then M points out that more than one film can be made of this Journey, so I try to let it all go. I think there is a pattern: daily opportunities to attend to prayer, amidst a myriad of experiences + daily distractions to draw us away from the essential.

We stop for horses, for rock throwing, for me to set a blessing rock upon a cairn. Lovely lanes. Hot hot sun. We pass a beautiful village, then stop for water. *O Santiago bless the fountains along the Way!* I read *The Pilgrimage* aloud (although we all much prefer *The Alchemist*). Some Spaniards come along and we learn there are 15 regions to Spain and four languages (not merely dialects) and that the word for twins is also the word for binoculars! To see further, powerfully. Yes, I smile and nod. Also the younger woman tells them, "it is good you are on the Camino for two months, the more time the better". We continue, with the boys ahead of me, talking about cartoons and books and Star Wars and inventions.

There is a practice I learned when we lived in Hawaii called Dynamind, (by Serge Kahili King) so, I bring my fingertips together as if holding a globe, then say, *"There is love and peace and harmony and happiness somewhere in my body, and that is good. I want those feelings to grow and spread."* I tap 7 times on my thymus, 7 times on the webbing on the top of my hand between thumb and forefinger on each hand, and 7 times on the 7th cervical vertebrae as I inhale with my attention on the top of my head, and exhale with my attention on my feet, this is the *piko-piko* wave breath. Then I breathe again with my attention focused, top of head and base of feet. Within three breaths, I feel so much more internal space, more ease ..

Heat. *Peace Love .. Peace Love ..* The contrast of deep shade. Many streams and a river .. all with plenty of stones merrily plonked into their deeps by the boys. Uphill and down .. lovely lanes like yesterday .. Birds composing arias about Springtime .. vivid green baby leaves on trees .. flowering apple trees .. huge bumblebees. We are reading Shakespeare's *Julius Caesar* aloud as we walk, talking about Caesar and the arrowing Roman roads, remnants of which underlie parts of the Camino. The boys and I try to mimic some of the birdsong. Hot. Hotter.

All three of us visibly wilting. And then we sight a whitewashed building, and coming into view, an ancient (Roman!) arched bridge. Down the hill we go, sustained by hope, and the increasing roar of the river over a weir.

Just at the end of the bridge, the albergue! Stepping out of the heat into the cool portico. Heavy old doors with beaten iron hinges .. art as hinge .. Ring the bell, wait, compare watch time with posted hours .. One of the doors opens, and the breath of ages flows over us. The man, whom we never see again, has us step into the cool darkness. A flight of stairs in front of us, to the left a small door. He opens it and as he gestures us in, the man says "*tranquille*" and motions us to sit. Two tiny worked leather chairs, who knows how old. And a small soft sofa. The boys sit happily on the sofa, the man steps out, closing the door behind him, and there on the wall behind is a huge old old painting of Gaudalupe! We last saw her in Paris, at Notre Dame. Oh she is so beautiful!! In a few minutes a sweet-faced little round elder appears, and he stamps our credenciales. We pause while some other pilgrims come in only for the *sello*, the stamp, not to stay. Then he closes the outer and inner doors and leads us into a huge semi-dark room. The quality of holiness is tangible. Carefully, we follow him into the room adjacent.

I wish I understood all of what he is telling me. The altar is, well, it makes me weep. A tryptich, a five foot sculpture of the patron who ordered it on the right, the saint of Navarre on the left, and the center is Jesus, with a heart surmounted by a cross on his chest. He is touching it. And then next to him is who? It looks like another man or a saint who is facing Jesus. This has been a pilgrim's refuge since the 11th century. The altar is more recent, yet the entire room resonates so profoundly with faith and Grace .. my heart .. my heart .. I can only respond to our guide with smiles and tears.

Then we follow him through other semi-dark rooms and into one which opens in one direction to the outside. He explains the locks, in case we want to go out that way. The other door is open to a walled garden. As the boys dart ahead, our guide tells me this is where the horses, cows, and animals with the pilgrims are stabled. Then we too are out into the sunny garden. Very high stone walls. Green grass, daisies everywhere. White chairs, scattered against the green. Several trees, some flowering, providing shade. Happy bees. At the far end, the old stone dormitory where we will sleep. Hello sanctuary! The boys spend the next several hours chasing lizards along the stone walls. There are also two cages of canaries to coo at and they are given a tour of the kitchen garden .. yes, a small door opens betwixt this garden and that! And I contemplate the altar in this garden from my place in the dappled light and am deeply grateful for the peace, this blessed sanctuary. *O thank you Santiago* ...

Imagine that you are made of Light, of Spirit.
There is nothing you need to do.
There is nothing you need to be
except what you really are.
Remember what you are,
and the dream of your life will have no limits.

Don Miguel Ruiz

TRINIDAD DE ARRE TO CIZUR MENOR

We slept so well in that place of deep peace. Outside it is 7° celsius compared to yesterday's 30°. Overcast. Quiet. We come out the side door, closing it carefully behind us. I look out at the neighborhood and shiver. Just as we start, a young man, a pilgrim, appears suddenly, striding over the bridge, and walks with us through this neighborhood. Dark looks from doorways. I am grateful for our companion. Then, as the land shifts, and all is well, he, our pilgrim companion from Ljubljana, strides off and away. *Oh Santiago, please watch over that young man, that angel in form. May he be well, may he be at peace.*

So begins our day, as if we are carried from hand to hand. We soon come to the ramparts of Pamplona, only to have to hide amongst the stone crenellations to protect the boys from an entire group of hungry-eyed tourists wanting to "take" photos. They swoop toward the boys. So scary, frightening, mean! After they give up, unable to find the hidden boys, and go away, we enter the city gates and are paced for a few minutes by a lovely woman from Ireland. She is walking with a Spaniard named Angel! They are quickly gone, and then, really, seemingly out of thin air, appears a tiny old man, no taller than the boys! He proceeds to lead us, telling us in elegant Spanish the history of his beloved city. He points out churches and insists that we walk slowly and listen and look at everything. He leaves us at a church, telling us to remember that he brought us to see San Fermin. Then he is gone, in an instant. We promptly step into the church on his behalf. *May the mystery of this Way, the Camino, be a blessing to all who touch the River. Thank you Mary, thank you Santiago, thank you dear ambassador for Pamplona.*

Emerging, we cross the street and enter a park, often with passersby directing us along the Way, and we realize the elder had led us through .. that we have passed through Pamplona! A few more kilometres, of climbing the hill to Cizur Menor .. accompanied by two nuns. The valley widens below us, the dark clouds hold back .. and we arrive at our albergue, which is in the care of a woman who places people according to her innersight. Then, an afternoon of spiritual conversation with her and with a few others, each person sharing how they are feeling at this point on the Camino, plus an interaction with a man's revered old tarot deck, which, knowing something of tarot decks, I won't touch. Still, direction comes though .. *constellation, love, teach.* I think we are just having a conversation which is very interesting intellectually, until he starts to behave oddly, which is creepy. Coelho's strange pilgrimage experiences come to mind; I end the conversation by walking abruptly away.

Meanwhile, the boys are safely out of range of all this, feeding the turtles in the courtyard pond. This is followed by hot chocolates while watching a hailstorm that turns the ground white. Perhaps today is presenting me with a deepening of the river of consciousness, or with illusions. *Thank you Santiago for all you are showing me!*

We're free
to go where we wish
and
to Be
what we Are

Jonathan Livingston Seagull

Richard Bach

Cizur Menor to Obanos

One could never have guessed that this day would have us walking six kilometres further than we had 'planned', nor that we would be sitting in a 15th century room in front of a splendidly warm fire, with the last of the day's light streaming through the tiny poured-glass windows. We slept late, until 8am. Some French fellows we met later said it was because it was Sunday(!) It was also because it was pouring rain, and, we had gone to sleep ambivalent about whether to continue today or ask if we could stay and rest. We left at 10:15, a bit worried. All for naught for it is cold and overcast with only a gentle rain from time to time. Thank you Santiago!

Climbing and climbing through fields planted with barley (we think). A sense of wide open space. A peaceful lunch on the worn, wide doorstep of a lovely (locked) church, sheltered from the wind. I love the contented feeling that spreads out from me with each breath .. *Peace Love* .. *Peace Love* .. The Way leads up and up. In the last two kilometres, in deep slippery mud, the edge falling away down to my right, I am suddenly overcome with an aching in my whole body, and a powerful certainty that I have walked this part of the Camino before! I glance at my clothes, expecting them to look different than they do.

Onward, into the teeth of the wind. Huge modern windmills spinning with a strange sound, and, as we come to the top, it seems we are cresting the spine of a dragon. After we crest the hill, the body ache and the intense familiarity pass. Dark low clouds, grey skies. Deep green undulating valleys in both directions. A few hill villages (each containing one church plus a handful of houses) pepper the undulations. Ahead of us is a wide valley with our destination somewhere therein. Perspective is so magnificent. M wants to learn paragliding. It would be lovely to follow the flight of the graceful hawk we watch swooping low, unfazed by the force of the wind .. the hawk and the wind understand each other fluently.

So, we climb that last few metres to the top of Alto del Perdon .. (Please look it up, there is a fabulous sculpture there.) Standing in that wind, these words come to mind: *Freedom. Simplicity. Slowliness. Silence. Relief. Sharing. Spirituality. The Landscape of Mystery*. Then down and down, out of the wind. If not for the weather, I would have hundreds of photos of beautiful stone buildings and ruins and stained glass and statues we walk past .. ah well. The Camino astonishes me again and again with its abundance of beauty. We come to Uterga and find the albergue and don't like it .. but we are so tired .. but then .. then we get up and walk on.

As Thich Nhat Hanh says, *"The purpose is to be in the present moment and enjoy each step you make."* What an excellent choice! The boys and I feel ourselves so deeply connected to the Camino, not as the road underfoot, but as the holiness that it is. We have a sense of being outside of time, and quickly seeming, we find ourselves six kilometres on, coming into this pretty town of Obanos .. to this albergue with its smiles and fireplace and songs! Just now, outside, in front of the church, there is a beautiful gathering of folk who are singing a song to a young woman who is getting married next week. *Thank you Santiago for affirming so much for us today!*

Bidden or unbidden,
God is present.

As heartbeat,
As breath,
As sunrise and sunset,
As sustaining and suffering love,
As dear friend rejected or embraced,
God is present.

Desiderius Erasmus

.

OBANOS TO CIRAUQUI

This is the Strange Road indeed. We left Obanos after the boys played in the churchyard/ playground for an hour, using the playground structures as props for their elaborate imagination. We walk without stopping for breakfast .. oops. We could have all stayed even longer in Obanos, such a friendly place. Kilometres later, I realize I forgot to find Felicia of Aquitaine's church, or actually, the church her brother built in penance, and where he lived in prayer for the rest of his life. The Camino has so much history, heartbreak and epiphany etched into it.

Many locals out walking today, often with their folding umbrellas. *"Buen viaje!"* Cool, blue skies and clouds drifting. Lovely walk to Puenta la Reina. Those who wax eloquent about the beauties of Navarra bear listening to – rolling hills, olive groves, vineyards, scenic – reminiscent of Italy and Northern California to me. In Puenta la Reina we find a correos! A post office! We mail two kilos home! Hallelujah! Then, directed by smiling locals, we walk over the medieval pilgrims bridge and out into the countryside. It is very hot, so we pause to read a chapter of Coelho's book.

Then as we walk, we share our gratitude for what we like and love on the Camino: Say hello to everyone. *Hola!* Or *buenos dias!* Or *buen dia!* Be respectful, well-mannered. Soap leaves (paper thin slices of soap) are super helpful during the day. Zip-off pants-to-shorts "rock!" We love our sleeping bags. The padded waistbelt is wonderful. Although wool does not dry here, the underlayers are heavenly, and wool socks are the best. "Fleece" is great. Wash clothes first thing at the albergue or refugio, then the afternoon is free. We like watching for messages, like how someone is making heart shapes of stones, lovely to come upon beside the Way. We love the sight of red plastic chairs, signaling the presence of a bar/café. We have learned to place our order at the bar, to pay and take it to our table, to return our dishes to the bar. We know to order bocadillas, tortilla con patatas, ensalata mixta. Cola-cao (hot chocolate) and café con leche are helpful companions. We love feeling that we are learning some fluency in the culture of the Camino. We love the feeling of taking our backpacks off at every opportunity. Foot massages .. ahhhh. We love the fact that we do not know where we will find ourselves throughout the day, the richness of the unexplored, the comfort of the waymarkers of the Camino. So much to be grateful for!!

We pass through a village buttoned up tight .. except for an elder man in the square who points to the opposite corner, *"Estrella! Estrella!"* This is our first reference to the Camino as itself, as the Milky Way, the River of Stars. The Way of the Stars, the language of the Heart (yours, mine, theirs), the language of dreams (yours, mine, theirs). Just beyond, we see a gorgeous village, our destination (in three kilometres), Cirauqui. Lovely lovely walk along beautiful lanes next to young vineyards and old olive groves. On our last gentle ascent to the base of the village, just outside, to the left, standing sentinel on the ridge, are two huge dolmens! I would love to go visit them! They remind me somehow of the sculpture at Alto de Perdon. We climb up and up through narrow cobbled streets just wide enough for the three of us to walk side by side to the church at the top. Next to it, our albergue. It is run by an artist, a woman who has decorated the albergue beautifully, and who, to the boys' delight, has jenga and a miniature chess set to play with.

Later, we head back down to a playground the boys spotted on the way up .. they play merrily for an hour. A fellow on his cell phone smiles.

I say *"Buen camino!"* He tells me he's from Brazil, so I turn to the boys and say, "He's from Brazil, like Paolo Coelho." The fellow is startled and suddenly attentive, and tells us that he is travelling the Camino with Paolo's wife! I feel he is arranging things. Or perhaps he is her guide. Strange Road indeed!

Unless you leave room
for serendipity,
how can the Divine enter in?

Joseph Campbell

CIRAUQUI TO ESTELLA

W e have walked six kilometres .. time to contemplate fear, an old unpleasant thing about trusting my instincts and having things go badly. Instead of continuing that pattern, how about trusting this process, the Camino?! That strange man we met, with the tarot cards, keeps showing up: so now I face my own fears. The boys think of him as 'Coelho's dog'. Note to self: *stay centred, the Way amplifies imbalances.* And, I have found that *this wondrous Camino amplifies love and light and grace and ease.*

I do not note every prayer I offer, every blessing, every thank you to Santiago, as they are so fleeting, so numerous. They are each footsteps on the Way.

Beautiful day. Gorgeous clouds floating in the expansive deep blue sky-ocean. Red oriental poppies. Purple iris. Scotch broom. Heather with pale violet flowers. Daisies. Flowering apple trees. A bush with yellow flowers that smell like honey. Huge bales of hay. A cross on a distant hill. The boys and I delve into philosophy. T has been reading *Zen Flesh, Zen Bones,* so he brings koans out and we contemplate them while we walk. Here, Zengetsu, a Chinese master of the T'ang dynasty, wrote the following advice for his pupils:

77. No Attachment to Dust

Living in the world
yet not forming attachment to the dust of the world
is the way of a true Zen student.

A pause in Lorca, at the swingset next to the fountain. A diminutive elder woman peers out her doorway. A few minutes later, she comes out to sit on the bench beside her door, then she asks me if we are going to Santiago. "*Si Dios quiere* .. if God wills it", I answer. As we gather our backpacks, she goes back into her home and returns with a handful of walnuts for each boy, and then for me .. the moment becomes emotional and she gives each boy a kiss on his cheek, then wishes us well, "*Buen camino, Buen viaje*" .. her eyes brimming. We will offer a prayer for her to Santiago whenever we arrive there. *O Santiago, por favor, bendice la dama amable de Lorca.*

Hours later, a church ruin that fascinates me. It turns out it is an hermitage of Michael the Archangel. I am filled with love and gratitude for the insights and support of family and friends who are thinking of us, and I think of those who would make this pilgrimage if they could. *May our journey of Peace carry you also. May you too be blessed by the Camino. May you be freed from all that ails you. May you be well. May you be free. May you be at peace.*

We come to Estella, and I remember the elder yesterday, was he saying Estella and I heard "estrella" because I wanted to? Or because he was saying "estrella"? It was so remarkable because he was the only person visible in the village. Yet another unanswered question. Ah well, *blessings on that elder.*

The archaic image of the soul
is likened to treasure
hidden in the midst of the body.

Mircea Eliade

ESTELLA TO VILLAMAYOR DE MONJARDIN

Estella. We went for a quick walk last night to get a sense of this old town. Ten "antiques" stores! Several with those pleasing footed ceramic jars, glazed in pattern or color, (with Latin words on those which ring the high shelves of the *farmacia*). Had a moment of wanting some desperately! Even to the point of imagining carrying one in my pack, the absurdity of which made me laugh, and anyway, the stores were all closed.

This morning, I awaken to the complaining cackling of the French women in our dorm room, I think they started even before they opened their eyes. I told the boys later that I am grateful for how little we complain to one another, and even then it's mostly when we need to pause. We begin our walk today with the boys playing with boats in the fountain. Thoughts: everywhere we have traveled, in all of the villages, there is laundry hanging out, sometimes at almost every window. Also, there are so many places to sit, benches beside many doors, stone or wood. Such a lovely thing, to pause, to contemplate, to appreciate.

At a turn in the road, a woman appears, insisting we go toward Irache rather than taking the shorter direct route, and so we do, coming first upon a double fountain of water, and, wine(!). There is a vending machine with small glasses for sale. Beyond this is Irache, the site of an 11th century pilgrim's hospital, a 12th century church and a 16th century cloister. It is just the boys and I, so I play some of Handel's Messiah, the music emanating from the phone in my pocket. O technology! I am watching the boys then suddenly turn (am turned?) and get a glimpse of a central fountain in the monastery cloister. The door is open, so the boys, and Handel, and I step across the threshold, a pattern of stones laid on their sides. A monk appears and shows us the cloister. Again, the feeling of familiarity I had while climbing the Alto de Perdon washes over me. Perhaps within remembering is .. for me, the call to sacred sites. All have a quality of remembering to them, a remembering of past and future. *Blessings to Mary, who is not hampered by time, so can intercede everywhen.* Is that true for you too Santiago? The monk allows me to take a photo of the cloister, so generously, so patiently.

During this entire time we are the only pilgrims exploring these old walls, these worn stones underfoot. We offer our bows of thanks, then we continue, outside and along a high stone wall, 10 or 12 feet high, half a kilometre long at least. The boys drop their packs and scramble up to assuage our curiosity, telling me it encloses a huge field. Imagine! More than two kilometres of wall built originally by who? Monks? Pilgrims? And when? We continue onward, pausing for refreshment in a hotel. We are a bit incongruous in their tidy convention/meeting room, but oh the coffee and hot chocolate are helpful. Thank you Santiago! Then we continue over hill and dale, past a pretty village, then steadily climb to here, Monjardin. I am fascinated by the structure on the hill above us, a hermitage? No, we learn it was first a Muslim castle, then Spanish, now partly restored, and tempting. M is adamant that we climb up however many metres high it is, but first we will seek our albergue. Ah, here it is, quiet for now. The Dutch volunteer lets us check in even though we are here early. There is a playground just in front, excellent!

We return to a place we paused at just outside this village, the 13th century fountain of the Moors, housed inside a restored structure with two Romanesque arches and a wide flight of stairs leading down in. We stay there awhile, the boys investigating the salamanders in the water, salamander-guardians, in company with a lizard outside. Close study also of an ant colony. Solemn launchings of walnut shells filled with blessings. This is deeply restful for all of us, for when we are walking part of our attention is focused on our destination, even though we cannot see it. Now we rest and share what we have thought about whilst walking. Today, we talk about how deeds (good or bad) move out into the world like sound waves and how one deed/quality tends to create more of the same. Also the boys have a lively discussion of some of the Clone Wars as "usual" and some as "the new Way, love reprogramming the droids." We then collaborate in making a Cretan labyrinth (of pebbles) on the threshold.

In the village again, we see the couple I think of as Joseph and Mary, so pleasing! I have a conversation in French with another couple, and the albergue volunteer, about the power of the Way to transform people, and about how Spain and France are imbued with Christian culture. The Camino is so powerful .. I feel as if our life before this is further away than kilometres .. it is another when.

Thank you Santiago for this blessed journey!

Pilgrims are persons in motion
– passing through territories not their own –
seeking something we might call completion,
or perhaps the word clarity will do as well,
a goal to which only the spirit's compass
points the way.

Richard R. Niebuhr

MONJARDIN TO LOS ARCOS

Slow start; we are so tired. This is our 12th day of walking. We almost stayed, but could not once we thought about it. There is this sense of being pulled onward. Still, lying down beside the path never looked so good! And yet, every time we sit, or start to sit, there are so many ants! The day is blessedly overcast. Trees flanking the path for maybe the first three kilometres and then this lovely lovely valley .. as far as the eye can see, cultivated fields, something vividly green growing. Wheat? Barley? The fields are as one, edged by the wilder edge of the hilltops. And also, amidst the fields, small groves of olive trees and acreage of vineyards. Mind you, this is a valley some nine kilometres long.

Peace Love .. Peace Love .. I would love to enjoy this lovely valley from the perspective of one of the many songbirds. I wonder what it would be like to be one of the elders I see in one of the olive groves, caring for the trees, watching pilgrims pass year after year. It would be a good valley to be a part of as the only buildings are ruins, with a church/

castle structure anchoring one end, on the far side of us. The boys ask me .. *If your God appeared in form to you .. how would you meet God? With what integrity? With what thoughts? With what whispers in your heart?* Their awakeness brightens all. The valley ends, or, the Camino follows, a lovely lane through huge pink flowering bushes. Fare thee well sweet place!

Reading aloud while we walk helps, still, the hours stack up and the kilometres do not. Many many walkers whoosh past us, it seems like busloads, many without packs, maybe more than 50 or 70! They seem very businesslike. How many/few are pilgrims? The approach to Los Arcos is very unpleasant. Grim-faced people sitting on the edge of town. Narrow streets, dark. We reject the first albergue we see. Then, around a corner, we come into a pleasant church square with café tables. This feels better, we continue onward and out through the gate and across the river to another albergue. Ah, yes, this one. The kind, elderly Dutch volunteer tells us that this is a three-day weekend coming up and that many Spaniards have credenciales, which last forever, and can be used whenever, so that they love to walk and stay at the albergues! That explains why so few had scallop shells or large backpacks. We have walked 12 kilometres in six hours. So strange, why the Way drags sometimes, or why we do.

A lovely time spent with a shop owner who, thank you Santiago, had the brimmed hats we have been needing! We are rather tan-faced, (and hands), in spite of the sunscreen. People say the blistering rash on the boys' ears is a sun allergy?! So the hats are safari-ish but we are thrilled because we have been looking since Roncesvalles for sun hats! The shop keeper also has a wonderful smelling unguent, with arnica, to use for massaging our feet. We are so very fortunate. I start a litany of gratitude to walk with tomorrow. The kind man at the albergue gives us a small room, private, so we can sleep early. *Thank you Santiago!* That feeling of being supported is heavenly. Just watched Federer win, at the bar where we got a bite to eat, and, a few minutes of the Tour of Romania. I think we'll miss the 20:00 mass in the baroque church, so maybe we won't be exhausted in the morning. Now, to sleep. We find a small chocolate carefully left on each of our sleeping bags! *O Santiago, por favor, bendice a esta amable anciano dulce.*

Favourite machines: Lavadora /washer. Secadora/ dryer. Hot chocolate/coffee/tea machine. Cellular phone. The spindryer for clothes! It's small, maybe 1/3 the size of a dryer, marvelous! and the Dutch fellow here says he thinks they will become more popular in Europe again since they use so little energy compared to secadoras.

The goal of life
is to make your heartbeat
match the beat
of the universe

Joseph Campbell

Los Arcos to Torres del Rio

Slept so well! I dash back to the same place we had dinner last night for baguettes and cheese and jam for the boys' breakfast. The lady proprietor sends kisses for the boys. Downstairs, the same Dutch volunteer gives each of the boys pins for their hats and tells them they are good boys. The warmth of his gesture brightens the whole day! We have coffee and hot chocolate from the trusty machine. The vending machine next to it has a fascinating array of items for sale.

A lovely cold day. Huge grey and white clouds in a blue sky. We can see far and guess our destination to be one of the two villages we see, however, with the way the Camino turns and flows, who knows? My red Greek prayer beads, treasured and used for decades, are in my hand. *Click, clack* .. As we begin, this thought-pair comes up: *crucible, chalice* (left, right ..), followed by many prayers. Thinking of St Francis, who is said to have walked some of the Camino (he founded a monastery in Santiago de Compostela), I am accompanied by his prayer:

Lord, make me a channel of thy peace.
Where there is hatred, let me bring love;
Where there is injury, let me bring pardon;
Where there is doubt, let me bring faith;
Where there is despair, let me bring hope.
Where there is darkness, let me bring light;
Where there is sadness, let me bring joy.

Thank you Santiago for this beautiful day! Thank you for the kind Dutchman. Thank you for his kind words and gifts to the boys. Thank you for the sweet lady's generosity and kisses. Thank you for our strength, our ability to continue each morning, no matter how tired we are. Thank you for this smooth path, the ease we all feel this morning. Thank you for our curiosity, and for all we see and learn each day. On and on, my litany of gratitude sent like fluttering colorful ribbons out and out. The boys and I talk about crop circles (there was a photo pinned up in the albergue) and about teleportation and about the hidden skills and gifts that people can have, and about offering all to good. We talk about miracles and about some of the people we have met on the Way. *M's watch stopped keeping world time yesterday! Now it is keeping Camino time.*

We come to the closer village (which we first saw from our starting perspective). I am so uncomfortable here but we take off our packs and the boys play in the playground for a few minutes while I look at where we are. We have already effortlessly walked six kilometres! Must go away from here, onward. We quickly head out and away. Instead of going directly to the adjacent village, the Camino goes around and down and up to Torres del Rio. It's only 11:00! Somehow, we walked for only two and a half hours .. and we are here. It reminds me of time and space in Ireland. The Camino is circuitous, a flowing river .. with room for prayer, and admiration of the beautiful vivid abundant land. The vineyards are just leafing. The olive groves radiant in their grey green shimmery-ness.

As we follow the yellow markers of the Camino, coming into this village, we see an albergue. At exactly the same moment, an elder woman appears further up the (otherwise empty) street and shakes her head, gesturing behind her. We follow her lead, walking together for a few paces until she smiles, stepping into a tidy house from which emanates the sound of a violin, (her student she lets us know). She points out our destination, sunny and welcoming, this albergue. Even this early in the morning we are welcomed. *Thank you Santiago! Thank you for the ways you direct us again and again to our good. Gracias por su amabilidad!*

If you could hear this: the laughter and exultant shouts of six boys and a dad playing soccer on the concrete playground next to the church here. M and T have been playing, speaking Spanish, scoring, running nonstop for the last two hours! And on the heels of eight kilometres of walking .. uitwaaien! After yesterday's tired day, today has been a delight! Our rest day. I am so grateful for the blessings of the Camino!

Much later, we are sitting on the doorstep of the church of the Holy Sepulchre. They say it was built by the Knights Templar. It does feel like the work or idea of magicians or alchemists, of experts in working on more than one level of reality simultaneously. The caretaker appears and we go in, followed moments later by some pilgrims, so we pop back out and wait in the sunshine. Then a few minutes later we have our turn, just us and the lady caretaker. It's a wonderful still space. Tranquil. Deep. Clear. Easy to connect with the stars from here. M and T meditate. Then we each add sound: *om mani padme hum*, a personal hymn, *hallelujah*. I see the caretaker understands why we waited to have our time here. Many smiles all around.

At the restaurant recommended, the lady at the bar agrees to make a tortilla con patatas, and it's fabulous! The boys play with the deck of cards

offered. It is the same as the one we saw in a bar
in Espinal, used to play the Basque game called
'Mus'. Our attention is taken by the parakeets in
a cage. While the blue one narrates, the yellow
one slides the door almost all of the way open!
Which makes me gasp. The barman/owner comes
over and ties the door shut saying, in Spanish,
"one day that bird is going to get out and be free."
Metaphors abound!

Wake! The sky is light!
Let us to the road again
Companion butterfly!

Matsuo Basho

Torres del Rio to Viana

The day began with two huge roosters running toward us from behind a small stone building.. and then, they crowed! And we laughed delightedly! They then dashed toward some other *peregrinos* (pilgrims), and did the same thing. I guess they are the exit committee for the village! Of course the boys had to follow them to their roost, that same stone building, with a red feed container, several other roosters, rusting farm implements in the yard behind. Then onward, oh the light this morning! Award winning lighting .. liquid gold pouring over the countryside .. perfect shadows and magnificent contrast between high clouds and blue sky. Cinematic.

Cold. No wind. Perfectly lovely. For some reason, the hills are difficult today. We talk about how 'flat' in Spain means hilly, and how 'hilly' means mountainous. T and M animatedly discuss their latest inventions for improved flight. The land is drier here, white under its veil of green. Hillsides of something that smells like sage. Huge agave. Rockflowers with pink blossoms. Small cultivated fields, just ploughed. Small orchards, apricot trees already with green fruit. Something like kitchen gardens, small plots with lettuces and onions, but adjacent to larger tracts, some wild, some green, some just turned, with huge dirt clods. We cross a couple of streams, the sound of water is a balm to my ears in this aridity. A long pause at one of the beehive shaped old stone buildings we think of as hermitages. There is room in this one for the three of us, and a stone seat for two, so the fellows go inside and then tell me about it. T notices that the ceiling is like that of Newgrange. M wants to live here which is such a wonderful idea.

Newgrange accompanies me as we walk again.. thinking upon the long strange journey of evolution for this species. How much knowledge we have lost, and what strange new things there are, just in the boys' lifetime. Things. Things. Things. In contrast, here, in the countryside is the land with its myriad ideas of Beauty, Nature, Bounty. Buildings are rare. The hills undulate to the horizon. Impeccable proportions. Vistas reminiscent of Greece and Italy. I keep praying as I walk, for the world to heal. *Blessed Gaia, may You be well. May humans come to love and honour and care for You as they did long ago. May You be well, may You be healed.* At a stream, we stop awhile for the boys to enjoy discovering its music, rocks, dimensions, which they do "immensely". A bit later, coming to the outskirts of Viana, we realize we have walked 12 kilometres in four hours. This explains how it has been hard at times, but it is also a great comfort because we do so want to walk all of the way to Santiago, and to do that we need to walk some longer distances, but not yet, not yet.

I feel so far away from everything, everything elsewhere in the world, everything not on the Camino, as if we are in a different time and reality. It is also not unlike being in the grip of a film or theatre production .. it's not over until it's over, and, one has to get up every day and go on, no matter what.

We walk up and up; always the Camino goes through the oldest part of a town, up to the church. In this case, next to the huge church is the Plaza de los Fueros. We pause, and then carry on down the Calle Mayor, to this albergue. It is noon, we are the first to arrive. Triple decker bunks (!!!) ours, in a small nook. Showers and laundry later, we realize the panaderia has closed, and it's Saturday, so, no bread until Monday. We drift back to the Plaza and people-watch. T wants to cook dinner, but M and I tell him we can get everything after 17:00, after siesta. Guess what? Not so, says the sign. The mercado is closed until Monday.

We go sit in the church doorway, the Portico Santa Maria, the boys lying down in the sun. We realize we like church doorways very much. T wants to be sure we come back here, to this one. Next, into the café-bar San Juan, which is hopping. Full full full. Lots of napkins on the floor, the sign of a good tapas bar. We get a table outside and order at the bar. After eating, the boys go inside to watch a motorcycle race. I happily observe the plaza. I am reminded of a story I have read to the boys about a park in Japan.

Here we watch the packs of men and boys, the bevys of women, the young women in pairs or threes, the small children running and playing and riding bikes. Boys kicking footballs, and when they lose control, the ball is kicked back, effortlessly, nonchalantly, expertly, by men of all ages. An elder lady, in her dress and heels, neatly kicks the ball, a huge smile on her face. An elder man is whistling. How rarely one hears that anymore. Tourists passing though. Spanish tourists dressed up to visit this pretty village – such a lovely respectful gesture, dressing beautifully to mirror and honour the village, to mirror and honour one another's respectfulness.

At 13:00, they are all gone, the plaza empty. We retire to the albergue, to read, to play cards, to arrange for an early night .. filled with all we have seen and enjoyed today. *Thank you Santiago for the experience of this beautiful village, this beautiful community.*

Blessing of the Elements

Blessed be the precious and preserving air,
the breath of life, our inspiration and delight.
Blessed be the precious and preserving fire,
the blood of life, our warming guest.
Blessed be the precious and preserving water,
the water of life, our cleansing guest.
Blessed be the precious and preserving earth,
the flesh of life, our sustainer and our wisdom.

Caitlin Matthews

Celtic Devotional

VIANA TO NAVARETTE

Pilgrims are not anonymous, for they each have their backpack. In some places, people would look askance at those they would mistakenly perceive as homeless. Here though, there is also the identifying scallop shell, and the fact that we are walking the Camino. So many Spaniards go for walks, gallivanting along parts of the Camino just because it's lovely. There are also many other hiking trails marked, so we keep a keen eye out for the yellow arrow.

We leave Viana this morning after walking to the fountain in Plaza de los Fueros, oh that wonderful plaza! This off-of-The-Way-water-seeking leads us to a bakery, its windows fogged over. 7:30 in the morning. We push on the door, it opens! It smells like heaven! The most scrumptious croissants, and says M, "the best donuts ever in history"! Then out through an ancient gateway, past a brilliant modern park, tiny great benches. I love great design juxtapositions, old and new. We walk. It is already hot and dusty. There is a lovely moment when we are unsure of our direction and a cyclist appears *in that moment* and helps us! *Gracias Santiago!* Through a pine woods, which smells wonderful in the heat, reminding me of Greece.

Next, the outskirts of Logrono. Industrial complex. Along a motorway. Through vineyards. A stop for our credenciales stamps at the "border" of Navarra and Rioja, the daughter continuing in her mother's place. Hot. Hot. Rioja looks markedly poorer than Navarra. Into Logrono. Many nods and smiles from older women, one tells me it is Mother's Day here in Spain! Over the famous old bridge, into the old part of town. It's 11:30. We have walked nine kilometres and the albergue doesn't open for another two hours, and we don't much want to stay here.

Onward. M insisting. Our first reward, a lovely café, its walls lined with American blues and jazz memorabilia and a poster for a Gus Van Sant movie. We sit outside at one of the café tables under the trees in Parliament Square, splendid. Our pauses have as much meaning, and sometimes more, than our walkings. Onward. Out through the other side of Logrono. Along a main shopping street, our eyes slow us down. A stop into one of the candy shops, not a boutique, just sugar, gum drops, hard candies, etc. Walking again. Cars are so noisy! Then the Camino turns and we come to a wonderful park. Young trees make lovely shade on the cool green grass. A rill that is several feet deep, and almost two feet wide, curves through the park, water cascading down the steps in the rill. Open to the sky. Great for stick boats or leaf boats. This is absolutely the best part of the day.

Reluctantly, after a long happy while, we leave. Then along a walkway of several kilometres with shady birch or beech trees and several benches. Families out strolling. Couples. A few joggers. Families on bicycles. Cycling is a big deal here. A few pelotons and many small groups of two or three cyclists. Well, the walkway ends at a reservoir/lake and there are hundreds of people, fishing, barbequing, picnic-ing. All ages. No one goes in the water, but oh how happy everyone is! We three pilgrims are the odd sight, just as sunburned and hot though. A girl, maybe seven years old, follows us for about a kilometre, smiling shyly at the boys. We walk around the lake and through more vineyards, climbing up and up. It is so hot we must access our reserves of willpower and carry on. There is no turning back.

Then, the worst of the day, several kilometres along a motorway. Here my *Love Peace .. Love Peace .. * is challenged by my thoughts of how awful this stretch is, and why do humans blight the landscape again and again and again. This is an old sorrow of mine, hard to move away from, so, I put my attention on the chain link fence which is filled here with hundreds of crosses, woven in grass or twigs. Interesting. Are they there to honour the suffering land? The land which suffers as Jesus did, though mutely. A mirror for my thoughts of suffering appears: a trashed area, a dump adjacent to the motorway. The Camino continues across, so we dash across and we finally see our village (or so we hope) in the distance. Through vineyards, past irrigation ditches with their doors, like those in canals, to block the water, to release the water. My eyes rest on the cool running water itself, bright and shimmery under the hot sun. We cross another motorway via a bridge, which I prefer to dashing across the tarmac. Past the ruins of a pilgrim's hospital .. we pause to discuss sleeping there .. then up and up through the village, to here. There are only five beds left .. whew! We did it! 21.4 kilometres It's 18:00. I am so proud of us .. so many hot weary steps today.

Be happy
whenever you can manage it.
Enjoy yourself.
It's lighter than you think.

Sister Corita Kent

NAVARETTE TO VENTOSA

Next to the albergue is a café. We start the morning with the jovial companionship of two young men from Austria, aged 19 and 20 .. very cool in their Icebreaker shirts and their board shorts and straw hats (one a fedora, the other an Irish cap). They are delighted with the boys,and it's most mutual, so I step indoors for breakfast, whilst listening to the four of them laughing out in the morning's coolness. The day is cool grey and overcast, compliments of Santiago. The young men head off, wondering if they'll manage another 45 kilometre day! We are impressed and wish them well. For ourselves, we are looking only to go to Ventosa, 7.6 kilometres onward.

Walking by the church, in front, a huge *fronton*, a drinking fountain, with a bronze statue of a woman with a jug on her head walking away .. The church calls hello .. so I must go in and so we do, pushing the heavy inner door open into the vast dark stillness of a sanctuary. There are only two small spotlights on, the rest is dark, quiet, waiting through time. Stained glass windows float like rectangular rainbow stars in the dark high above us. As our eyes adjust, we move around a column toward the altar. The small spotlight shines on a life-size statue of Mary and baby Jesus. She has a dolorous face and an amazing crown of silver rays, and, behind her, rising up easily 60 feet, is an amazing work of 16th century art. Life-size sculptures of saints, smiling and nodding, watching us. Great golden columns, intricacies we cannot fully perceive. It's all golden, glimmering in the shadows, breathtaking. We are alone as humans amidst a company of great beings. We are welcome, benevolently so. Our first gasps of surprise and awe become candles lit and then softly sung "hallelujahs". *What is it like to be honoured for hundreds of years, in effigy, and, in eternity? Greetings Great Ones, thank you for your beneficence!* In Latin, *Gratias ago vos pro vestra beneficentia.* We remain in that liminal place for a long time, yet when we emerge from the church we are not sure how long we were there for we were truly outside of world time.

The rest of the day pales in comparison, seemingly ordinary, yet buoyant as the blessing of our time in the church imbues every step, for hours. An easy walk through a patchwork of vineyards, the occasional employees in their dark blue overalls. So many huge smooth rocks under the earth, and above the earth. M stops and builds a beautiful rock sculpture, so important symbolically. Again, I am struck by how each person's Camino differs. This sculpture, so powerful. Such a blessing to travel with these two amazing human beings!! Onward .. a discussion of backpack designs ensues, since ours need improvements. Oddly, the Camino is interrupted at the edge of a huge motorway, and we are keenly, intuitively, aware of the interruption. It is re-routed along the motorway, so we decide that the noise is that of transport vehicles and speeders entering and exiting a space port .. it helps! Then discussions of maps, of how differently the different stages are presented in different countries' guidebooks that we have looked at. We want one that shows the whole. One that perceives fully ..

Happily we arrive at our albergue, hours before it opens, and pass the time with local exploration, the boys off on their own, (but in my sightline), and a scrumptious lunch. Then, something lovely in a mortal, human way: two peregrinos, our Mary and Joseph, arrive at this same albergue. We are all heart-happy to see one another again. As I write, M and T are playing dominoes with one of "the darlings" as the boys call them, this sweet young couple, who are very present as pilgrims on the Way. They are sweet and kind to the boys.

It is a joy to spend time with them. The afternoon is chess and checkers and dominos betwixt them and the boys, many languages spoken, and a shared dinner prepared in the kitchen. (The boys made a delicious salad.) Later, a young woman sings fado, the notes aching. Also in the warm good-smelling kitchen, an older man, who is both pilgrim and seer .. what he says to me causes me to have the boys greet him .. that too is most interesting. *Gracias Santiago por todos!*

Your task is not to seek for Love,
but merely
to seek and find
all the barriers
within yourself
that you have built
against It.

Jalal ad-Din Rumi

VENTOSA TO AZOFRA

Today I am annoyed at myself for a while .. at feeling like we have to hurry to find a place. I know it's solely my own invention, this problem, but I still buy into it, or am today. *Please forgive me Santiago for my anger and impatience. Please help dissolve me into Love.* Rather than rush ahead of myself, I think of Thich Nhat Hahn, of this idea of being present for each footfall. So I slow, internally and externally, imagining the feet of hundreds of thousands of people over the last 800 years .. the bare feet, the different shoes, the strides of all, tall and short, rich and poor, honest and not, religious and not, spiritual and not, yet all, all passing this way. The earth feels every step, they are all written there, for eternity.

I also think about the countryside, about the elders I see, often alone in a vineyard or garden or field. Where are the young people? It makes me sad sometimes, but my regrets and sorrows are too heavy to carry, so I don't, hoping instead that they'll transmute into something in the landscape, something useful or helpful. The boys and I like the countryside best, lots of space. We talk about the life we left behind and cannot imagine how we'll shoehorn ourselves into that house, that life.

We come upon a small hillside covered with mounds of rocks, and with towers of rocks. Both boys build towers. They leave the walking sticks they found three weeks ago there. We pass the location where local tradition says the Spanish version of David and Goliath fought. Here they are known as the pilgrim knight Roldán and the Syrian giant Ferragut. I am thinking of myths and of histories. This is a story of two religions fighting. Quickly through Najera, except for a pause at a nice café. I am reading *The Pilgrimage* out loud as we walk. Everything comes to a halt, as a huge flock of sheep passes us .. the pattern of their days intersecting with ours.

We arrive at the refugio and of course there is room. I think there always will be room.

Laundry, and observation. Thinking about "the darlings" and other kind, open-hearted pilgrims and volunteers and townspeople we have met. Contrast this with the prying pushy types who usually are American or Canadian, with no sense of respect for others' privacy, for ours. Is it their egos? Is it their natures? Is it the relative youth of the current form of their countries, the short-sightedness? Here, where traditions are those of hundreds of years, we learn again and again that common courtesies, *daily manners, daily small gestures of respect, are the bulwark of civilization.* We are experimenting with how to respond to these pushy types, to those lacking civilized reference points in their behaviour. First we were polite, but that oddly seems to encourage an almost aggressive line of questioning. We so very much wish peregrinos and paparazzi types would respect our requests for privacy. They take take take photos, greedily, but do not give .. anything. These last couple of days we have been simply not responding or staring or being abrupt, but this is not the tone that we want for ourselves, nor for our journey. We want to model what I think of as the Graces of civilization: kindness and tolerance. There must be a way to be graceful and peaceful in the face of these unwanted attentions. *Make me a channel of Thy peace. Make me a channel of Thy love.* Most folk from other countries (other than America and Canada) usually want to just ask the boys if they are having a good time and then they wish them well or tell them that they are brave or strong or some such compliment .. then they go onward .. respecting us, respecting our space, as we respect theirs.

A German fellow last night was telling me how much he is enjoying his journey because every day, and sometimes every moment, is different. He calls this the *Camino of a Thousand Faces* .. isn't that lovely?! Joseph Campbell would smile.

I feel that I am walking out of my old life and into a new life .. one that I cannot yet imagine. I am at a place in the ocean where I cannot see the shores I once knew so well .. their beaches and rocky stretches fading into the mists of time past. I am concentrating on the immediate, and cannot see my destination .. thus I become aware that I am held in God's hand ..

God
is the absolute reality
underlying everything

Emanuel Swedenborg

Azofra to Santo Domingo
de la Calzada

Hot late start. An elder lady gives the boys each bamboo walking sticks! How wonderful are the blessings of the Camino! As we climb out of the valley, lo and behold, a golf course with a private clubhouse. They let us in! Lunch, and space.

Thinking so much about the poem we saw painted on a wall outside of Nàjera yesterday, signed by 'E.G.B.', and which has proven prophetic ..

Dust, mud, sun and rain,
is the Way of Saint James;
thousands of pilgrims
and over a thousand years.
Peregrino, ¿Quién te llama?
What mysterious force attracts you?
It's not the Milky Way,
nor the grand cathedrals.
It is not the Navarran courage
Nor the Riojan wine
Nor the seafood of Galicia
Nor the land of Castilla.

Peregrino, ¿Quién te llama?
What mysterious force attracts you?
Not the people of the Way
Nor their rural ways.
It is not the history and the culture
Nor the cockerel of la Calzada
Nor the palace of Gaudi
Nor the castle of Ponferrada.
Everything seen in passing
Is also a glimpse of all
Yet the voice which calls me
I feel more profoundly.
The force which pulls me on
the force which is attracting me
Does not explain itself, nor can I.
Only He in Heaven knows.

A slow, brutally hot day. All day we have been dealing with the heat, and then .. the brutality of traversing a ghastly huge creepy empty abandoned housing development.

We gain strength by reminding ourselves of the Cistercian convent where we will stay tonight .. but when we arrive, the door is locked, they are not accepting any pilgrims at this time. We all weep.

Peregrino, ¿Quién te llama?
Pilgrim, who is calling you?

In the universe,
there are things that are known,
and things that are unknown,
and in between,
there are doors.

William Blake

Santa Domingo de la Calzada

This is a different missive. I would have it arrive joyously but that is not what is happening with me just now on the Way. There is an irony to the amazing experience we had in the church, and my current thoughts. What I have, what we three have, experienced in the last two days, not today, is a Camino that has been redirected to follow alongside roaring stinky busy hot motorways (!) And it is being trod by tourists with backpacks. The quality of history and hundreds of years of pilgrimage has too often been absent and instead it has been as tiresome and dead as a shopping mall. So, then you add in walking through industrial areas and trashed areas and an entire housing development that was utterly empty, and I have become increasingly disappointed and sad.

It is a big mistake on the Camino to take this sort of reality personally, but I have been. I miss Navarra! Add in hot hot days, and longer days of walking because of the pressure to get to Santiago by a certain date. Also add in that we had to stay at this new, clean soulless albergue, which would be fine, but it wasn't what our hearts had longed for all day yesterday. So, it was too much for me and I cracked and ended up last night with some sort of a sun allergy that looks like sunburn but with huge swelling of my face, and hands, and feet(!), and a fever to boot. I have seen others suffering with this, but didn't see it coming. Fortunately, since I could not walk at all this morning, the elder French volunteer took pity on me and let us stay. I am weepy, but not from joy.

Oh, the sandpapering of my personality! I have got to find my enthusiasm again, change is afoot, and we are in the River indeed! I feel like I have lost my courage to continue. I have been trusting the boys to the kindness of pilgrims and the French volunteer and his wife all day, since I cannot get out of bed for most of the day. This too is a huge sandpapering for me. *I have so many places of density, will I ever get through them all? Through .. to the Light?*

Late in the afternoon we go out and buy flowers, and chocolate from a gorgeous jewel of a chocolate shop to give to the French volunteer and his wife, who gave us the boon of staying. We step into the cathedral, to see where the famous chickens are, the chickens who proved Santo Domingo's miracle-working a thousand years ago. The

current ones are there. The cathedral is solemn
.. mass is beginning .. I am reminded of Julian of
Norwich, and the power of the great Mystery. Her
words: *All shall be well, and all shall be well, and all
manner of thing shall be well.*

Now, outside our windows, downstairs, is a
rehearsal for the 900th festival for Santo Domingo
de la Calzada. The children are solemn and excited
and practise and practise, again and again. Thank
you Santiago .. this is for you, isn't it?!

I insist that our contemplative work
shall not be directed up or down,
to this side or that,
forward or backward,
as if it were a machine.
For it is not the work of the flesh
but an interior vital adventure
pursued in the Spirit.

The Cloud of Unknowing
14th C. by Anonymous
(translated by William Johnston)

SANTO DOMINGO TO BELORADO

Now THIS has been an interesting Strange Road day! More about logistics than scenery, or more about quantum mechanics than art. We awaken at 6:15, due to the lights on in the room and the morning rustles of plastics and backpacks. Am grateful for all of the loving thoughts from family and friends over the last day. Surely they have helped me heal in body and spirit. *Thank you, thank you!* My feet aren't swollen anymore so we are out and walking by 7:00. Lovely cool morning. Walking across the bridge and through the fields, storks nesting on special platforms and on chimneys. Happy with the cool air. We sight Granon, the village I had been thinking we'd stay in tonight. As we come close to it, the road forks, the Camino signs indicating down a steep hill toward the motorway. Yet, from our vantage point, we can see that the Way then heads up another hill into the village, so instead of down and around, we go straight, past the cemetery into town .. and *we can feel, as well as see, that this is an older road,* even if it isn't the current waymarked route .. so wonderful to follow our felt sense of the Camino!

We head for the church and find a café for *desayuno*. The two cafés are full of peregrinos. When the boys go dashing off to explore the village, the café lady tells me (in rapid Spanish) how it is good to have geraniums and petunias in the doorways and windows to keep the mosquitoes away! Must try it. I did notice that the geraniums' leaves here are wonderfully pungent. Since it is not even 11:00, we decide to aim for the village eight kilometres on, Viloria de la Rioja, the birthplace of Santo Domingo as well as the location of a small albergue for which Paolo Coelho is the patron. So, onward, the heat rising. We stop in the next village and contemplate their albergue and decide to continue on. In the next village, the shop is opened by a woman who is just returning from errands. Lucky us! Strawberry ice creams help the boys along.

O the vast sky!!! The swallows darting, the sky full of their swooping calligraphy. One alights, the shining blackness of its wings reminding me of ink, of Chinese calligraphy, the idea of a perfectly placed brushstroke.

All through the region of Rioja, the open-air raised stone and cement acqueducts (O Roman Empire!) adjoining the fields are being replaced with kilometres of black steel or iron piping. Why?

Much digging of trenches and widening of lanes. M speaks into one length, half a kilometre long, and hears a wonderful echo. We walk to the other end and then he waits, timing a message, then he and his brother send a loud "hello" through the pipe just as some oncoming pilgrims walk by the far end. It works! The group stops, looks around, the boys send another "hello!" There is much gesticulating and then they point toward us (for I have inadvertently given away the game by standing near the boys).

As we are walking into Viloria de la Rioja, a car pulls up and the woman driving it hands me a card for her albergue in Belorado, nine kilometres further on. No way can we walk there in this heat after so many hours already walking. A Brazilian couple, E and F (she of the fado singing several nights ago), are waiting outside the Brazilian albergue at which we too are planning to stay. It is closed, not surprising for mid-day. T and M build a bench in the shade, which is much appreciated by all! We all spend the next two and a half hours talking about the Way and generally having a lovely time. No bars or cafés here, and we are all hungry, so we share the nuts and chocolate we have. E reminisces about the last time he walked, nine years ago, and how the Camino was much more spiritual and religious then. He gives the boys each a pin from that Journey for their hats! Then, still, the albergue is closed. The sign said it would open at 13:00, but it's now 15:00. So, they decide to continue. We cannot, so we three adults manage to call a taxi using their guidebook and cell phone. Our friends walk on. The boys and I sit in on their bench and wait, while I read aloud about waiting (in *The Pilgrimage*). An unmarked Mercedes pulls up, our taxi! The woman driving it gets out and chats with a woman who appears from the house facing us. It turns out the Brazilian albergue owners have gone to Santiago de Compostela!?!

It is notable that we still remember how to climb into a car, and, how strange it feels to do so. Down the hill and then we whoosh the few minutes to Belorado on the motorway. We see the Camino has been (artificially) moved alongside it, so we are spared kilometres of that! As we are zipping along, I feel like we have come off of one plane of the Camino into a 3D grid .. as if we have taken flight and are in the Milky Way. Amazing sensation. Almost instantly, we are at the albergue and yes, it's the one I was given the card for earlier!! Private room. Fabulous, like the best rooms in the taverns of old. Again a sense of now being on a different time-space version of the Way. Also, as if we are not yet here in

Belorado. An intense price negotiation, resolved, followed by a stroll to the main square. Orienting. Orienting. We flow in and out of two cafés and then into the third, and who is behind the café bar?! The taxi lady!! We have accomplished in one day what I thought would take three. Now we must sleep, and savour this opportunity to not be in a crowded room of strangers.

Ah, the taxi! A "thing." Does it sully the purity of our pilgrimage? I think not, knowing there have always been conveyances (animals or animal-drawn carts and carriages) along the Camino. I could not see another way except to sleep in the ground in front of the albergue with no food or bathrooms to be had for kilometres. (And thank Santiago we didn't do that, for there is a huge rainstorm that started an hour after we arrived safely in Belorado.) Nope, the Way of Suffering is no longer relevant, and indeed detracts from the consciousness change we are attempting as a species. So yes, having thought about it, I regret it a bit, from a perfectionist rigidity, but standing on principle would make this, the rest of this pilgrimage, a grim prospect. We are more than 200 kilometres into our Journey and we have more than 500 to go. For us it feels far better to be light-hearted, curious, free, open to serendipity ..

Early to bed. Last thoughts .. *M and T and I are being handed from caring person to caring person along the Way .. so watchful, so gentle, so thoughtful .. Gracias Santiago!*

To romanticize the world
is to make us aware of
the magic, mystery and wonder
of the world;
It is to educate the senses
to see the ordinary as extraordinary,
the familiar as strange,
the mundane as sacred,
the finite as infinite.

Novalis

(Baron von Hardenberg)

BELORADO TO VILLAMBISTIA

We slept so well as a party of three in our own room. The boys slept until 8:00, unheard of because that is the exit time for most albergues. Further wonderfulness for them was hot showers, and cartoons in Spanish. So here we are at almost 9:00, stepping out the door onto the street, and coming around the corner are E and F! We are all equally shocked and surprised and so happy to see one another, our "dos amigos" says T. They had been walking this morning from where they had stayed last night. So, we must all go have breakfast together. We go to the taxi lady's café/bar and laugh at this unexpected gift. E teaches the boys a magic trick, and after breakfast they show us caves in the cliffs behind the church. People have homes in some of them. They remind me of the cave houses V and I saw along the Loire near Chinon years ago. So we walk, with grand plans for many kilometres of walking. We are all, M and T weighing in as peers, so busy talking about Buddha and Ayurveda and energy and the seer and what he told each of us. E wants to stop and look at everything that interests the boys, so we float gently along the Way. E tells us about leaving a stone, (with one's faults to be absolved of held in the stone), at the Iron Cross near O Cebreiro, so we spend some time finding volunteers among the quartz sparkling around us. We come upon huge hay bales and the boys must climb them, E willingly also. Thus we ramble, delighted in life, each other, the many expressions of beauty and nature ..

When we come to this village, Villambistia, we stop together for lunch, which ends up being a stop for the night. The albergue couple also run the only bar in the village, so there are the card players and standing groups of coffee drinkers and everyone smokes constantly and the bar has room for three small tables and yet sometimes there are 20 people standing in there, laughing and talking. The albergue's peregrinos-of-the-day are on the periphery. Everyone observes everyone very closely. It must be grand for this village of 50 to have this daily influx of peregrinos, to observe over coffee and drinks, and then go home. Because our friends snore, they are moved to another room, an office, where they won't disturb other pilgrims. The boys and I have a look. Next to it is a big (well, it's the same size as the bar, but empty) diocesan classroom and meeting room. After a quiet discussion with the proprietors, the boys and I move over here. Light on three sides.

Space. Mattresses to put on the floor. Fabulous. The boys read (a James Herriot book and a sci-fi book). I meditate, such a blessing! I arrange for an early dinner, a Basque dish of tuna and potatoes and bell pepper and onions and bay leaves. Yum! The idea was to go to bed at 19:00, well, the local singers gather in our room! It's their once a month practice, and they fill the room with music! We wait downstairs in the bar. There is a huge thunderstorm. The bar gets more crowded. The oldest villager is maybe 90, the youngest, a tiny baby. There are several toddlers in the mix, fascinated by the boys. After the singers leave, we go upstairs. The bar goes into full swing, and it's loud and happy until the wee hours, so, not much sleep for me, but it's wonderful to listen to people so happy .. laughing and laughing. *Gracias Santiago for this day of friendship and music!*

Rise,
and drink
your bliss;
For all
that lives
is holy.

William Blake

Villambistia to Agés

We awake to a freshly washed world. We are worried a bit because supposedly there is a 12 kilometre stretch without any albergue or cafés. Staying here means it's a 17 kilometre day which is hard to face, that matter of choices made yesterday impacting today. We know we want to get beyond Villafranca which is just five kilometres on, so, we walk. Our dear dos amigos, E and F, travel at their own pace today. The rain stopped at 6am, and now, at 7:15, everything is so gorgeous. The colours of the earth and vegetation are vivid and luscious. The stone buildings and patchwork stone walls look like art, pleasing in their subtle colour shifts from white to pink.

At the edge of the village is mud. Ah yes, our shoes soon have that two to three inches of thick mud that makes walking slippery and gooey and heavy going. Villafranca and breakfast are suddenly not an easy walk away. So, we distract ourselves by singing silly songs, and doing multiplication tables, and admiring the view. We try to spot the birds who are singing so merrily. Then, just as we crest a hill, Villafranca comes into view (so helpful to sight one's goal!) and we come upon a ruin of a 12th century monastery, a 30 foot cube with the roof fallen in and flowers growing on top of the walls. Very singular in the landscape. Who lived there? And did the Camino then go straight across the river and onward over the Montes de Orcas?

We turn left and walk on the shoulder of the road to Villafranca (and desayuno). Now my wretched, oft-inaccurate guidebook says it's up and down steeply to San Juan de Ortega, and that there's no water to be had betwixt here and there. And 12 kilometres is such a big number, but we don't want to stop here! We have only seen two other peregrinos this morning, but here at the bar we watch 20 arrive in twos and threes. Onward. Behind the church, the path becomes a narrow track and up we go, up and up, pausing to catch our breath and notice the perspective changes looking back down over the valley. Montes de Orca is a wilderness area, protected. We come to a view point with picnic tables. The track widens to a narrow road width, easy for the three of us to walk abreast .. *Peace Love* .. *Peace Love* .. Oak trees with small trunks, two hands could span most of them. They are mossy with orange and yellow lichen, their pale leaves from last autumn are underfoot, no new leaves yet.

And here is what happens .. we come to another rise, not as steep as before, and the road widens and we find ourselves walking more and more easily and faster and faster! We can tell we are on top of the mountain, but can only see the oaks on either side. The road widens until 20 could walk side by side. The sun is drying the mud but we must make our way carefully, over the slippery parts. There are many many peregrinos walking. It gets hotter. We keep to the shade on the edge and *we imagine the Way as a great wide river undulating over these mountains, mirroring the Milky Way, the peregrinos as fish, each in their own part of the river, the Way.*

It gets hotter and the oaks are suddenly replaced by pine, which smell wonderful in the heat, and remind me again of Greece. We walk faster still, as if we must. It is easy for us. Wide, wide and only one other hill, a drop down a ravine to a bridge and burbling brook then back up along a hillside of purple, like huge heather? A purple allée, then back into oak then pine again. The boys and I have a wonderful philosophical discussion with extensive religious and spiritual and arcane sidebars. We count bugs, shiny round big black beetles with blue iridescent bellies. 53 in all. We estimate it would take one of them a year and five months to walk to Santiago from here.

Then we are descending to San Juan de Ortega! We are full of energy and so pleased with ourselves and, thrilled to sit down. We put our packs in line. We have walked 12 kilometres in three and a half hours. The albergue is part of a monastery church complex. Oh splendid serene church. Magnificent carvings on the columns. One, of Mary, is mysteriously illuminated at the vernal and autumnal equinoxes. Painted stylized dragons or serpents on the ceiling. Fleur de Lys. White stone. So so lovely and cool.

A shout – they are letting us check in. So we do, and the hospitalero opens a room for us, bunks next to the window. The room quickly fills. We do the usual – wash laundry, hang it to dry in the inner courtyard. We wander about, split a bocadillo at the bar, and it comes out that the boys really don't like this place and want to leave. There is a mass at 18:00 so we will nap for an hour and decide. At 17:30, I am startled awake by a voice commanding, "*Rise up and come to me!*" There is no one in the room except the boys and I. An intense felt-pressure to continue onward. I awaken the boys at 18:00, massage their feet (as I do every night) and ask them how they feel (without telling them what I heard). Yes, onward! They feel an urgency too. We are out at 18:15, past all of the shoes piled at the door, fleetingly regretting not being able to say goodbye to the pleasant young man who checked us in. Hurrying. Onward. Instantly certain as we step outside that this is correct action.

The evening light is called the magic hour for a reason .. the rays of the setting sun pull us forward .. and we walk with such ease, feeling such lightness .. to the next village, Agés, pleasing in the lovely light. The prettiest grassy churchyard with a stork nesting on the belltower. The two albergues are next to each other. No beds available together. Now what? It's already 8pm! The woman of the municipal albergue and bar comes up to me and says she has seen the boys and has an idea, their new building(!) with our own room. *Gracias por todos, siempre, Santiago!* And pasta made just for the boys while we watch a soccer game in the bar. She wonders if the boys will come back and see her when they are all grown up. She foresees great things for them both. How wonderful and extraordinary a day!

Christ has no body now upon the earth but yours.
No hands but yours, no feet but yours.
Yours are the eyes
through which Christ's Compassion
looks upon the world now.
Yours are the lips
with which His Love speaks now.
Yours are the hands
with which He bestows blessings now.
Yours are the feet
with which He walks doing good now.
Christ has no body now upon the earth but yours.

St Teresa of Ávila

AGÉS TO BURGOS

Of course we slept in .. and got up and packed slowly and trickled over to the café to return the key, and to have brekkies. Sadly, it was dreadful, but fuel nonetheless. So, onward, *ultreia!* A wonderful old stone bridge. (Am still enjoying everything made of stone!) We meander along. Rural Spain is SO scenic .. valleys of green, stone walls, trees, butterflies. It is startling to come to the villages sometimes, mixtures of ruins and newly built houses, dirt tracks and paving. And they button up! Shutters closed, and strands of plastic in the doorways so one cannot see if the door behind is open or closed. In the Basque region, often they were strands of metal twists (think licorice sticks), and since then we have seen plastic brown versions of the metal, and now all colours and styles. Often one pushes through them to access the panaderia or mercado or the bar/cafés. Thus, each person makes an entrance, crossing a threshold blindly.

We have walked through so many villages (small here is 25 residents or fewer) and have not seen a soul. Well, always cats or dogs. But no people, or, one or two elders in their garden plots, bent over their short hoes, working away amidst rows of various vegetables ..

We are in a wide valley, low hills to the left, a protected area .. the village of Atapuerca is in front of us. This area is where the oldest human remains have been found. 900,000 years old! (We leave the Olduvai Gorge out of the conversation for now.) We look at a drawing of what they thought such a human looked like on the poster leading into town. I tell the boys that humans and chimpanzees are 98% the same. M promptly asks how current scientists can be so certain of evolution; what if chimpanzees are devolved humans?! He and T elaborate on this. Hmmmm... We stop for a better breakfast in Atapuerca, off the Camino. The panaderia/ mercado/café/bar is next to a playground, and better yet, has an adorable small dog who looks, and plays, like a puppy. A long happy pause later, we climb out of the valley.

Today is the second day I have just wanted to collect rocks. Nevermind this walk, look at all of these gorgeous rocks! I cannot imagine how a geologist could bear it, maybe walk slowly and just think, "quartz, granite, limestone"? .. a different kind of prayer. I wish I knew what it is, this, these rocks, smooth white or roughened with lichen, in angled ridges. They say the hill is full of caverns. This rock is most compelling – of course folk settled here 900,000 years ago! We climb a narrow sheep track, perhaps also worn by pilgrims, and at the top there is a 40 foot cross with a huge pile of rocks at the base, excellent placement with the sky as backdrop. Just beyond is a huge flat area (think multiples of football pitches) where someone, or many, have made a spiral using stones. Very nice so close to the sky. We had hoped it was a labyrinth though. Nice juxtaposition with the cross.

As we come to the edge of this flat mesa we can see Burgos in the distance. Good grief, it's gigantic! First though, down the hill, the boys running (with their full packs) into the wind, a stormfront trying to push us backward but they run under it. I happily lean and walk. And then we are down the valley to a small village, buttoned up tight. No bar/café. No albergue as promised, (wretched guidebook). There is a lovely Roman fountain at the far end of the village, so we pause .. but there's nothing to do but push on. The next village is the same. Here though, both the bar and the albergue have signs saying "cerrado". Bother!

We are wilting badly, so I promise the boys and myself, "the next car that appears, I'll ask for a lift" .. this, even though we haven't seen one for hours. Not two seconds later, a car comes around the corner! Now I'm in it, so I wave him down, promptly forget all of my Spanish, and nonetheless, he gives us a ride to Villafria. Such a relief on the boys' faces, mine too I'm sure. Seven kilometres in five minutes. Shocking .. and such a blessing! He drops us off at the bus stop and I give him a pin I have worn since we began our Camino. I had already planned to take the bus the last eight kilometres into Burgos, as many peregrinos do since the Camino here has been bulldozed and it's an infamously ghastly walk .. think of the worst suburbs/industry/misery. The bus we need to take arrives not five minutes after that angel leaves! *Thank you Santiago!*

As we motor in, I think about villages and cities, how the villages are blank on the outside but the action is inside or in the inner courtyards. The city is full of window displays to encourage people to go inside, to, what? Buy things? The bus driver lets us off near the flamboyant statue of El Cid. We walk along and into a lovely park. Fountain. Café at one end. People sitting on benches. Then around the cathedral, scenic, mega-baroque, and we arrive at the albergue (euro modern, very nice). At 20:00 we are in a huge bustling café off of the Plaza Major. Lots of napkins on the floor mean the locals like it. This followed by a four hour (!) wait until my turn for the dryer (for our laundry). Then to sleep, 100 peregrinos on five floors, dreaming ..

We shape our self to fit this world
and by the world are shaped again.
The visible and invisible working together
in common cause,
to produce the miraculous.

David Whyte

BURGOS TO TARDAJOS

Nice place, the new albergue. Out by 8am, and then where for desayuno? We start this drifting turning oddness that will still see us in Burgos five hours later, as if we are in some maze. Strange drifting in circles around the cathedral. First to Plaza Mayor which is closed! I mean all the cafés are. Different hours here than the villages. Different people, more closed faces, more fear, more caution. So then around again .. and we find an open café. Then, the boys are on a mission to find some game cards they want, but the shops don't open until 10 or later, so we drift and circle again. *I remember Ariadne's Dance of the Cranes, Daedalus' labryrinth. What are the gods trying to show me? What is Santiago wanting me to see here?* The Divine is present, but in my absence as we drift and turn, I am neither whirling like a Sufi, nor walking in meditation.

I suggest the cathedral .. we pay to enter, tour groups all over it .. scenic, but chilly and unfriendly. Still, Santa Ana's chapel is wonderful wonderful. We light some candles for loved ones.

The cloister is serene and so pleasing to me. Out again .. beggars at the door and thieves roaming the plaza outside the cathedral .. so say the many posted signs. We stay alert, very alert. "They say that pickpockets see only pockets and saints see only souls." Lori di Mori's words rattle in my mind. Then looking .. looking in many shops for what the boys are seeking. No luck. An unexpected investigation of a sword shop. Very interesting for the boys, who have never seen real weapons of any kind. The shop also sells mechanical birds which I admire. We each get a souvenir. Then we fetch our packs, which we had put in lockers .. and now we have to get lunch, and oooof .. finally we are walking out of Burgos!

In a park, I see one of the beggars from the cathedral doors chatting happily with a friend in a park .. which shifts my attention, my vibration, my heart, my awareness, up and up. O thank you Santiago, for your direction! *Por favor, bendice la gitana de la catedral!* Out through the ragged edge, familiar poverty, and a shop with what the boys were looking for. Two happy boys! Helpful people are showing us the way! Oh yes, this is good! Onward, past an hermitage, a university and more suburbs. A flock of university students is studying surveying ..

There is the dirt path! We feel like we have walked forever, like Burgos is trying to hang onto us .. we keep walking .. stop to rest for a couple of minutes .. keep on, keep on .. looking for the town with the albergue. A new path next to the motorway (hello daft planners), and just then, an elder on his bicycle goes past, arcing across the fields, yet ending up where I think we will too, so we go thattaway. Hot! Past a scrumptious wide river and a stand of trees. We drag ourselves into a village .. Tardajos! However can it be? 10 kilometres that hurts like 100. We are exhausted, feeling like we are dragging, feet and legs in agony .. trying not to cry. The tiny albergue is full upstairs. The lady is thrilled to have such young peregrinos so she opens another room .. Four beds. She is so wonderfully welcoming! And F and E are here! Thank you thank you thank you Santiago! To bed, as M says, *"to walk the Camino of Dreams"* ..

Mastery is power
over oneself
that is created
by three things:
an awakened Heart
Self-discipline
and,
Self-control

Hazrat Inayat Khan

TARDAJOS TO HORNILLOS

Our sleep was so restorative. Breakfast outside, compliments of the hospitalera, for all of us, at 7am. Cold, breath in clouds. It feels like camping. Everyone is bleary-eyed, with soft smiles. Birdsong. Purple irises. Café con leche, or hot chocolate, and toasted baguette with jam. Our Brazilian friends, F and E, want to walk with us. It is such a beautiful morning. We sing many songs as we walk out of the village and then up into the fields. This is the *meseta*! Slightly rolling hills, then flat, planted with wheat of barley or oats. We walk higher .. the green meets the blue sky .. I am so happy .. I could dance .. a sea of green vibrancy .. piles of white stones .. a few trees, as punctuation to this essay on abundance. There are so many birds singing and crickets and even a sleepy owl once. Small wildflowers. The eye looks to the horizon. Hallelujahs! This is the landscape I first dreamt those many years ago! I am astonished and deeply happy, every molecule of my being sings, my soul cries out in joy! Happy happy!

In a village, a home with blooming cacti in the window, an old man at the door. At F's happy "Hola!", he smiles warmly and gestures, inviting us in. A room like a museum, old stone mill wheels in another, but there is no more water for them. He is so lovely and grateful for our enthusiasm, and we are so honoured to be shown his private sanctuary. It makes me want to come back, to ask all of the questions that I have, of all of the elders. *Santiago, por favor, bendice el dulce cuidador de recuerdos.* We continue, animated by that sweet man, feeling so grateful. The boys are observing the huge ants on the Way, and naming them. We are passed by swarms of peregrinos and tourists with backpacks .. including twenty-odd on bicycles and the same amount with daypacks (their luggage going ahead). Only a few minutes today without other people in sight, completely different from our other days so far.

We come to Hornillos before noon. The albergue will be fine. A happy lunch with our friends followed by a visit to a shop. *Helado* (ice cream) for the junior set. A huge shaggy dog wakes up from his nap, greets the boys with smiling eyes and a waving tail. The afternoon includes, for me, a vitally important span of time (and eternity) in the church, staring up at the beautiful statue of Mary .. high high above the altar .. *O Mary, thou art*

Our Lady of Loving-kindness. Thank you for watching over all of the children of the world, the children of all ages, of all species. The warmth of your love is a balm. Thank you! Let me be a channel of thy love, thy grace. Thank you for all you give, to so many.

Someone in the albergue tells me there was a huge prayer circle and a mass in Roncesvalles a few days ago .. prayers for the world .. and that so many people came from all over to be part of it .. How beautiful and wonderful. I imagine bouquets of flowers, the radiance of love in those prayers delighting the world.

Be it known also
that insofar
as anyone is in the stream of Providence,
so far he is in a state of peace;
also that insofar
as anyone is in a state of peace
from the good of faith,
so far he is in the Divine Providence

Emanuel Swedenborg

Arcana Coelestia 8478:4

HORNILLOS TO HONTANAS

The meseta! Fierce wind. 40°. Storm clouds, which Santiago ever so kindly moves south of us. A vastness so incredibly majestic and magical. M and T and I, three motes in eternity. Ocean of green meets ocean of blue with towering clouds. Powerful. Two hours of this, then we feel, and promptly take, a side path, down a narrow valley, to a thousand year-old spring, older surely, but known as a source of healing waters for some thousand years. An unexpected encounter: a peregrino we last saw two weeks ago who came here and is now volunteering here as hospitalero! It is a place of wonderful qualities of peace and charity. E and F appear! And a sweet German woman. We all crowd around the tiny table in the teensy tiny kitchen .. lovely .. warm and cozy. Then a young couple comes in and joins us .. ooh like angels they are .. so radiantly lovely .. the internal Flame illuminating their faces. The boys and I are delighted to see them. They are camping and walking the Camino. The young man says he started his pilgrimage in Ireland. I understand completely! There are binoculars, so the boys take them outside and look at the hilltops. Then, we all gather for a water ceremony .. an exchange of blessings. Reluctantly, the boys and I gather our packs, say our fare thee wells, and continue back up and out of this sacred valley.

Up onto the meseta again. Huge piles of rocks, seemingly random .. some recent .. some older. A tractor in the distance.

Then a valley suddenly appears and tucked down on this side of it, a beautiful worn village, appearing like a gift, a surprise. The municipal albergue is on the main street, on the Way, medieval in origin, wonderfully restored. The boys insist we stay, T says, *"the energy is so loving, from God, and from the heart"*. All afternoon, we bask in the peacefulness. A house on the main street is being renovated, so several village elders gather and watch the work. One elder man decides to give each of the boys a gourd, as the traditional pilgrims had! There is much washing and preparing and threading of twine, with the help of the hospitelera .. so so wonderful, such a gift! Then we walk out to the edge of the village, 250 metres says the sign, a municipal swimming pool?! A delightful couple proudly offer us freshly made fruit salad, and cheese panini, sitting beside the swimming pool (spring fed, open in June, reflecting the clouds) ..

so many different birds singing .. and swallows, darting to the water, skimming it, with ripples and splashes. This entire day a gift for which we are so grateful! The last of the sun warms the lilacs, perfuming the air.

[He] was beginning to understand
that intuition is really
the sudden immersion of the soul
into the universal current of life
where the histories of all people are connected,
and we are able to know everything,
because it is all written there.

Paolo Coelho

The Alchemist

HONTANAS TO CASTROJEREZ

Lovely brekkies at the piscina, with the sweet young couple who own the café there. Thoughts about the weaving of the pattern of the Way on the part of the village folk who run the albergues. They know it all, have seen it all. Watching the pilgrims come and go, discerning the difference between peregrinos and tourists. This poolside hour of contemplation is followed by a lovely walk along the valley floor .. lovely weather, thank you Santiago! We come to the ruins of San Anton, and, there is a tour bus. This is the worst part for the boys, those times when a group becomes a fiendish horde, grabbing at them, and taking pictures of them. So mean! We deliberate whether to go forward or wait. We run the gauntlet of their cameras, me mirroring them by taking rapid constant photos of them, their faces so startled and affronted. Maybe they'll think on this and be less greedy in the future. Oh it makes me so angry. So we wait by the roadside until they drive by in their coach. Then we stroll back, and look at the niches where bread used to be placed for passing pilgrims. And then, I argue with a French photographer (with entitlement issues) who wants to take pictures of us. To have us pose for him. "Take" is his verb. So rude.

I release my anger, slowly, *left, right, left, right* .. *Peace Love* .. as we walk along another valley to Castrojerez. A monastery to the left, church on the right, castle ruins on the hill. The bells toll noon as we come into the village, such a confusing map. And then a joyous cascade of bells, as a carillon, as if someone was in the belltower laughing and dancing. We pass the church and see children in special regalia. Folk coming from everywhere in the dusty village. We continue on, thinking we'll come back to the church to investigate, not yet knowing the village is two kilometres long! We come to the albergue recommended by the couple at the piscina. It is owned by a young man, who walked the Camino twice, and then came to this place .. and has been restoring this house for five years. He gives the boys half of his lunch, his tortilla, the eggs from his hens .. so generous!

Later we walk out to the convent of Santa Clara and have .. an extraordinary blessed experience .. *Gracias Santa Clara! Bendice a todas estas santas monjas.*

Afterward, we come down .. off the holy mountain as it were, and contemplatively walk back into the village, and try to find food. Because of the *feria*, everything is closed. Standing outside the closed mercado, we are at a loss. I turn and see a woman watching us. In Spanish, I explain we need food .. she wonders what kind, so I say bread and cheese. *"Aspetto uno momento."* She goes in her house and comes back out and nods .. and unlocks the shop door, opening it for us. Thank you Santa Clara and Santiago! Later, walking by another house, an older woman comes out and shows the boys two baby Siamese kittens. A long happy pause on her doorstep, as you can imagine.

Then it's 19:30 and M insists we climb up to the castle ruins (9th century). I want to cry at the thought but will not deny him. So, up we go .. up and up a narrow track. Very strong winds. Desert dry. Scrub. White stone. Dirt. Precarious switchbacks. We do arrive at the top and the boys' joy makes it all worth it! Much clambering and happy investigation ensues. Am reminded again of how much vastness they have, and of how I am too often constrained by fear. Much to contemplate as the wind clears my mind. Hello view! Such beautiful land, such a delight to see so far! Down again, a different goat track than we took going up, with less of a drop this time .. still, it's not until we reach the village that I can relax. So, we didn't get blown off the edge today .. all is well. *Thank you Santiago!!*

Make the universe
Your companion,
Always bearing in mind
The true nature of all creation –
Mountains and rivers,
Trees and grasses,
And humankind..

Matsuo Basho

Castrojerez to Ermita de San Nicolas

First thoughts: Aaaaaaargh! Trying to deal with Germans. There have been too many instances of grabby-snatchy-piggie-wiggies for me. This morning a German couple wakes up and speaks so loudly they awaken everyone else in the room! Then they snatch most of the breakfast items (leaving all the rest of us to share very little), and leave without doing their dishes! Ooof! Further, this seems to be the long Wednesday of this trip, neither here nor there. In addition to that, the thought of another month of albergues and sleeping among strangers is disheartening. And, so many men, many shopping for company .. tiresome. And so many flipping questions .. snarl! Anyway, enough of that. So, solutions: I do all of the dishes and clean up the kitchen while thinking nice thoughts. I will made a point all day of being extra nice to all peregrinos, especially all non-photograph-'taking' Germans as an apologia for my closed heart this morning.

We have desayuno and the young hospitalero introduces us to his huge exuberant dog, the size of a St Bernard, but yellow like a Labrador. A last-minute call for a backpack courier service. The fellow who appears embodies happiness at this service he provides, which is his way to live well and communicate with many villages along the Way. I insist that he take the boys' backpacks, an idea which they are not comfortable with at all. We are all having knee problems due to backpack weight – that 10% of body weight maximum exists for good reason! As it happens, I keep picking up rocks .. and postcards and other ephemera. We keep hoping for a correos. The one in Castrojerez was open M-F, but only from 9am to 9:45am! We have hopes for one in Fromista! We are in need of a rest day again .. thinking of taking a train or a bus for a day to move ourselves further along and also to rest.

Seeing that they are feeling strange without their backpacks, the hospitalero gives each boy a necklace with the scallop shell on it. Then, with farewells to him and his splendid dog, off we go, both boys now relishing their freedom. We could see our route last night from the castle ruins. Out of this place and into the unknown .. and so glad to be on our way. Walking along a bit of old Roman road. Emperor Augustus traveled this road, with his retinue. I understand this to be part of the Via Aquitana linking the gold mines of Galicia with

Rome. There are other stretches later along the Camino that are better, longer, more evocative .. still, we are here and Charlemagne too was here. Would love to look at the relevant maps! Then uphill, like last night, but a wide dirt road. Part way up, M insists on taking my pack, and then he fairly gallops up the hill! Leaving us panting behind him. He won't give it back, and it weighs a ton, I know! Instead he waits for us at the top, at ease, comfortable, strong, happy, taking in the view. SO strong! The Camino seems to strengthen him every day. And he has dashed up ahead of, and faster than, three deeply impressed young Germans and a Spanish cyclist .. the latter is saying "*Bravo!*" to M when T and I arrive. Whew!

The rest of the walk is effortless, even with my pack, across the top of the meseta, where, as T said, *"I am taking in everything, the wind, rocks, trees and much much more."* This the last such meseta. Coming down, now the landscape is called "tierra de campos", the land of fields. Low rolling hills, or flat. Trees where there is water .. different species, many cottonwood and alder, an occasional lone olive, also almond and apricot. I think of 18th century romantic landscapes, they were painting what they were seeing indeed! *Peace Love Peace Love.* I look to the right and see a church tower, our village perhaps? Then to the left, 50 huge modern windmills on the far hills.

We crest a rise and see below us a beautiful stone building with a lovely garden and flowering trees (purple flowers), and beyond it a Romanesque bridge, and a wide river. As we come closer, we take in the flowering rosemary, and red roses next to the walls with more rosemary. I feel like I am seeing a medieval garden, with herbs of restorative properties .. and, and more than meets the eye. This is the hermitage of San Nicolas. It doesn't open until 14:30 and we have to find the boys' backpacks in the next village, two kilometres further on. We want to stay and wait; how I regret letting their packs go ahead/away from us! We drag forward, over the bridge and to the village. Coming into the bar, yes, they have our backpacks, and they assume we'll stay, but no, the boys are off like lightning, running back toward the hermitage! I have no capacity, so sit to have some soup .. our friend F is here .. solo (?!) After a few minutes, I begin to fret about the boys, so I too am off, albeit walking, not dashing like the boys, back toward the hermitage. Just as I leave the village, a fellow comes up behind me on his black ATV, engine roaring. I wave him to a stop and ask him for a ride to the bridge. No problemo. I clamber aboard. Rumble to roar, me holding my walking stick, arm outstretched .. rumbling against the tide of oncoming pilgrims. Thirty or more. Interesting. Did they not see the hermitage as they walked past it? Or is there a crowd awaiting beds? Are the boys alright? I am so uncomfortable! Meanwhile, my steed is fabulous! Jouncy and unstoppable. It makes me laugh out loud. At the bridge I clamber off, and the fellow bows (!) then rumbles and roars away. With thoughts of knights and armour and honour, I cross the bridge, so grateful to that fellow, so grateful for speed.

Crossing the bridge is like coming home .. the boys are contentedly sitting on the bench out front. I am filled with relief. Old stone, old stone. Later I will learn the hermitage was built in 1100 and that it has been a church, a pilgrim's hospital and a military outpost over the years. Also, that this side of the river, centuries ago, was Christian, and the far side, Muslim. The Italian hospitaleros arrive. One looks exactly like S. Nick! There are eight beds. We are 12. The last two to arrive are German, and quick to grab beds, rather than politely wait to be assigned places. Snarl .. I mean, "think nice thoughts." The Italians put the boys and I in bunks (even though they want to sleep upstairs). A bit later it transpires that the two German women won't budge and another German man refuses to sleep on a mattress on the floor because he says he has reserved (obviously he's a tourist, not a pilgrim). So, one of the hospitaleros, his kind face full of worry, comes to me .. could we sleep in the loft upstairs?! (Which is where the hospitaleros normally sleep.) Oh yes! Happily! Mattresses on the floor for the boys, a bed each for myself, and one hospitalero, and F, who has appeared! Perfect! We can look down along the long table to the altar with its Russian icons of Mary and Jesus and St. Nicolas and San Jacobus (Santiago).

Private. Quiet. Refracted sound. A small window toward the bridge. One even smaller above the altar, this enveloping hug of stone, this serenity. No electricity. Of course the boys and I tell one another how very much we want to live in a place like this. When I come outside and see the labyrinth etched in stone by the door, I can only laugh and sing hallelujahs. Laundry, hand pump, cold water, cold wind. (This is the coldest springtime in 20 years. I have worn my gilet almost constantly.) The boys are outside playing and investigating all afternoon, me too. Such a wonderful place! An elder man comes and cares for the garden .. he smiles at my delight in it. Oh .. we could live here .. we could .. we could. All afternoon, locals drop by, casually. Each just happened to stroll two kilometres (each way) to see who's staying at the hermitage today. We three have not enjoyed an albergue's energy of this kind since Roncesvalles.

I am so grateful for the deeply peaceful beautiful garden, for the boys laughing, for the strength of this hermitage. The Italian hospitaleros are preparing dinner. 7:30pm. The bell is rung. We all (now 15) come in to the room, candlelit!

Transformation! Two hospitaleros have on short cloaks with scallop shell decorations. We all sit on the chairs placed for us in a circle on the altar area .. and then .. there is a ceremony of having our feet washed! A prayer in Italian is recited for each person, the two hospitaleros kneeling, *"in the name of Jesus and this Order, may this ceremony give you the strength to get to Santiago de Compostela"*. I tsk tsk the Germans to put down their cameras, (they do). When the circle of washing is complete, there is a moment of powerful energy .. I gather it and offer it up to God. Then we rise and sing a patenoster and an Ave Maria .. deep breath .. hearts have been opened. We step down from the altar and take our places at the long table for a candlelit dinner. As we sit, there is a whoosh of energy as the angels come into the space .. candles flicker. A few minutes later the door opens and in come three people, a playful funny local fellow, who sits across from us, and an Italian couple from Perugia. She brings homemade cheese to share with all. Places are made .. a gorgeous delicious dinner .. oh we are such lucky peregrinos! The man from Perugia wants to talk with me about Mary as the Mother, and as the Virgin. Much later, the boys and I excuse ourselves and go up to bed .. listening to the others singing folk songs and hymns, and lastly, a lullaby ..

In a dream I walked with God
through the deep places of creation;
past walls that receded and gates that opened
through hall after hall of silence,
darkness and refreshment
- the dwelling place of souls
acquainted with light and warmth -
until, around me, was an infinity
into which we all flowed together and lived anew,
like the rings made by raindrops
falling upon expanses of calm dark waters.

Dag Hammarskjöld

Ermita to Boadilla del Camino

A candlelit breakfast .. oh why do we ever eat by any other light? "The air is crispy cool which gives everything a mystical touch.", says M. A young German comes to sit next to me. He needs to tell me he awoke in the middle of the night and went out to look at the stars! Ah, beautiful! I can see them in his eyes .. equilibrium restored .. perfect. The boys use an old jam jar to make an ant home. Then, last of all, we must leave. Oh no! Please, can we stay forever? But we must go. The three hospitaleros come outside to give us hugs. An emotional moment .. tears .. open hearts. All three of them stand outside waving and waving as we cross the bridge, we too waving and waving, until we are out of sight to one another .. sigh. Onward, *Ultreia!*

As we come to a rise, T says, "I had an interesting idea. What if everyone was made of glass, with the sun shining through them?!" Ineffable .. I am speechless at the beauty of that idea. After that, there is only philosophy; the three of us share our loveliest thoughts with one another as our feet find the Way, unerringly. More clearly than ever, it is obvious that no two people experience the same Camino. T and M and I overlap in our Journey, and for each of us, this is a unique and irreplaceable experience.

Coming into Boadilla del Camino, one of the boys finds a stork's white feather .. which symbolizes purity, fidelity, renewal and longevity. In Ancient Egypt the stork was associated with the soul. Our albergue has a beautiful courtard. We sleep tonight in a converted barn, in the former hay loft. The edge of the loft is marked by a huge beam hung by ropes from the rafters! There is a blind pilgrim here with a companion .. such compassion, such courage ..

The privilege of a lifetime
is being who you are.

Joseph Campbell

BOADILLA TO CARRIÓN DE LOS CONDES

We are thinking of walking to Fromista to get to a correos and then taking the bus to Carrión de los Condes. Knees and ankles hurting, not good. We have desayuno here, and we are told there is no direct bus, that the only way is to take a bus to Palencia, 25 kilometres south, then up via another to Carrión! And, he says we can catch the same bus from here in 10 minutes, so yes, we'll do it! An adventure?! We walk around to the bus stop, watching the road eagerly. Well, the bus arrives an hour later! It's tiny! It seats ten. And, it promptly goes right through Fromista!! So much for that correos idea! Past the fascinating 18th century canal locks, part of a restoration plan, drat! We would have loved to investigate those. Clacketing across the land to Palencia. A huge statue of Jesus outside on a hilltop. Oh, it's a ghastly huge city! Shocking! Cannot figure out the point of being here.

My solution is a church. There is one nearby, the 14th century Iglesia de San Pablo. A long pause first to watch the old men playing bocce ball. Then the boys investigate a square with exercise stations. They are experts on Spanish playgrounds at this point, always trying out everything on offer. One of the stations is to exercise the arms by tracing huge infinity symbols. Fascinating! Into the church .. a beautiful spotlit statue of Mary. Everyone nods to another statue of Mary, one with a man kneeling at her feet. So blissfully quiet. Everyone else is an elder. Well, maybe the candles we lit here are the reasons to be here?! We step out into the bright sunlight. And, the church is locked behind us .. hmmm. Thank you Mary for that time in that sacred space! Next, a lovely lunch at a café outside the church. We shoulder our packs again and return to the bus station.

This time the bus is a deluxe tour coach type. As we fly across the land, I see storks nesting in the belfry of a ruined church. Every church for days, since Azofra, has had storks nesting. They symbolize so much good. We get off the bus at Carrión. A woman passenger insists on giving me kisses and wishing us well. *Santiago, bendice a la señora cariñosa!* The refugio is around the corner, at the monastery of Santa Clara. Within 15 minutes of our arrival, it is full! whew! The boys catch a darling lizard, who they name Pumpkin, and who they first put in their unused ant jar, but who ends up riding on one or the other of them as we explore the town. We meander all of the way out to the former Benedictine monastery, now a hotel. Stands of poplar trees, and cottonwoods with their white fluffiness. Dinner near our refugio, at a marvelous bar, filled to the rafters with old men, smoking, playing cards, watching bullfighting. We sit outside. The boys return little Pumpkin to where they found it; its pilgrimage complete. They wonder how it must feel to Pumpkin to have covered so much ground from the height of their shoulders or hands ..

I am thinking to maybe not write for awhile, instead, to get through this.. this wanting transformation or change and not finding it yet. I walk past the refugio entrance.. seeking ease. I check to see if the Santa Clara church is open so late in the evening. It is! And .. as I open the door, I hear prayers. To my right, the nuns are behind their grille saying Hail Marys! Respecting their privacy, I quickly look away and sit down facing the altar. A few minutes later, the boys come in, and, except for a 15-second foray in by two local children curious about the boys, no one else comes in. 45 minutes of prayers and beautiful beautiful hymns. Such exquisite singing voices. Whatever is it like to live so? To have daily hours designated for prayer. Do they ever get cranky? With each other, or the world? Their music elevates all, it ripples out across the town, Spain, the world .. *Thank you Santiago! Thank you Santa Clara!*

It is not we who seek the Way,
but the Way which seeks us.
That is why you are faithful to it,
even while you stand waiting,
so long as you are prepared,
and act the moment you are
confronted by its demands.

Dag Hammarskjöld

Carrión de los Condes
to Terradillos de los Templarios

A pleasing desayuno at Café Espagne. The bar lined with men smoking and drinking coffees, one eye to the television. A group of four laughing over ringtones. Am thinking about all of the variations on "Buenos dias" there are: Buenos dias. Buenos. Buen di. Buen dia. Beuno dia. And the "Hola" variants: Ola. 'La. 'Laaaa. Of course everyone greets everyone, entering shops, leaving shops, passing on the street. Wonderful. Am also noticing .. everyone is so old! Where are those who are 20 to 50 years old? We see a few, but so few. War? Franco? A question I'd ask if I was deeply fluent, but if I was I would probably already have discerned the answer. Sigh. It makes all of the villages a bit sad .. a sense of waiting or longing .. and who will people these villages, large and small, ten and twenty years from now?

Glad we wandered about yesterday to the Benedictine monastery, past the poplars, through the main square, looking in shop windows – all of it – because today, we left the Santa Clara convent and had desayuno and then went to the correos (which we had located yesterday) and spent an hour(!) getting a box organized. Three kilos. Pray that the statue of Santa Clara and the two calabazas arrive in one piece! Magnificent to feel our load lightened. Then to the mercado for cheese and bread for dinner, and back to the bar by the refugio, which is the bus stop for our conveyance.

Whisking through space, we descend at Terradillos. Carrión was a relative city; this town has empty buildings and a full albergue. However, the lady offers us beds on the floor in the restaurant – after it closes. No problem. But does this mean we must always arrive at our destination by noon? Also, am noticing how many albergues take reservations. So where do pilgrims go? I wanted to stop here because it is the literal halfway mark between Saint-Jean-Pied-de-Port and Santiago de Compostela. Also, it supposedly used to be a stronghold of the Knights Templar. Would've been nice to sleep outside. Again, like Palencia, this makes no sense. We notice that we regret a bit of what we did not walk, but we also feel strongly that we must not only go to Santiago, but beyond to Finisterre. Must say, it is hugely disconcerting and unsettling to travel by modern conveyances. So, to reorient, we trace the Camino we have walked on a huge map on a wall at the albergue. We are thinking about what we want for the second half of our Journey along the Strange Road, wanting to articulate it clearly. Tomorrow we walk to Sahagún. It will be interesting to see how it feels after two days of bus travel, even though total time aboard was less than three hours in two days. Now the boys play with the albergue's cat while we wait for dinner to be finished, etc. so we can get to sleep. My guess: at least another two hours. *Thank you Santiago,* not all days are comprehensible I see.

We all want progress.
But progress means getting nearer
to the place where you want to be.
And, if you have taken a wrong turning,
then to go forward doesn't get you any nearer.
If you are on the wrong road,
progress means doing an about-turn
to the right road;
and in that case the one who turns back soonest
is the most progressive...
going back is the quickest way on.

C.S. Lewis

TERRADILLOS TO SAHAGÚN TO ASTORGA

Wake up in the restaurant, having slept so well on the floor. Have desayuno and walk. How thoughtful of the restaurant owners to care for the pilgrims. Though not a luxurious stop, still, we were all, eight of us, warm and dry and safe. Just outside of town the road forks. Which way shall we go? An old man on a bicycle appears! *Thank you Santiago!* Both roads go to Sahagún he lets us know. We take the road now less travelled into the countryside, past an old Camino marker. Hot. Pause at an abandoned hermitage ..

Then into Sahagún. Dusty, hot, not appealing. I spot the train station .. we clamber through a semi-locked gate and across the railroad tracks (after some diligent looking and listening). First train please? No, not for Léon .. first beyond. Astorga? Yes! That feels perfect.

A 40 minute wait, contemplative, curious. Then we whoosh across the land, only two hours instead of the three we were told it would take.

We are accompanied by M's Marcus Aurelius, Book IV.25:

Think of the number of things, bodily and mental,
that are going on in the same moment
within each one of us;
and then it will not surprise you
that an infinitely greater number of things
– everything, in fact,
that comes to birth in this vast One-and-All
we call the universe –
can exist simultaneously therein.

Astorga .. up toward the cathedral. We always head that way don't we?! First hostel is iffy, though pleasing in a 60's communal way, colourful and friendly, with some familiar faces. They open another room. Okay. We check in and get settled, then off to explore. Excellent salads at a café on the cathedral plaza. Looking for flipflops, we end up across town. Roman ruins, mosaics .. and there, across the street, another albergue. We decide to stop in to check it out for tomorrow, since we have just decided to stay here in Astorga for two nights for a bit of respite. We are met by such a welcoming fellow! Good light, clean, "wonderful!" says M. We move today, now, dashing. Quick stop into the cathedral as folk gather for 20:00 mass. A good day for prayer. Then we check in at the wonderful albergue. Stamp our credenciales. I dash back to the first albergue to help a woman's knee while the boys wait at the cathedral. Run into L and his mom. L, a new priest, fervently believes that suffering is the only way to validate the journey .. so I tell him, *no al sufrimiento!* No to suffering, instead, offer your joys to your God. His mom smiles, then I do, then .. L does. Later, all of our dashing about breathlessly behind us, finally, finally, bed.

T shares this parting thought from *Zen Flesh, Zen Bones*, specifically from *Centering*, (a Sanskrit manuscript more than 4,000 years old), Verse 10:

> *Eyes closed, see your inner being in detail.*
> *Thus see your true nature.*

If the doors of perception were cleansed
every thing would appear to Man
as it is, Infinite.

William Blake

Astorga

We awaken to a friendly hospitalero telling us it's fine to leave our packs on the beds, and that we can return any time after 11:00 as they wish to tidy the albergue now. So wonderful to be free of the pack weight .. we feel like floating! I remember the delightful man of his "camino of a thousand faces", and I think, ah, this is a camino of a thousand days .. that "thousand" expands and contracts as needed by each peregrino, and, each day could be perceived as a camino unto itself. I look at today, this day's camino .. oh Astorga is a good lucky place to be today!

I want to go to mass at 11:30, and, as we wander the plaza, I hear a workman telling an elder that mass is at 10:30 not 11:30. *Is it an angel who sharpens my hearing to catch those words across the plaza? Thank you!* By 10:15, the benches on the plaza are full of elders. At 10:30 the cathedral gates open and we go in, taking places on pews. The service begins and I think about world peace. *Peace. Let there be Peace. Bless this beautiful world.* Then my attention shifts to the busybody next to T who is crowding him terribly, and I am nearly halfway off the pew myself. She has been assigned to speak and afterwards is so proud and happy that she takes up even more room, fluffing her feathers like a chicken. This would be charming if it wasn't so uncomfortable. So I give our three seats to two elder ladies knowing they won't get pushed around. We go to the back of the church where it is empty. T sits on the floor in the centre of four huge columns. Light suddenly streams upon him. A beautiful moment. M says happily, "We saw the portal open!"

Our souls
should be like a transparent crystal
through which
God can be perceived.

Hildegard of Bingen

ASTORGA TO SANTA CATALINA DE SOMOZA

We stop in for breakfast at the same café as yesterday and watch the mechanical clock strike 8am in the Plaza Mayor. Then we return to the first albergue, where we didn't stay. *Thank you Santiago*, my walking stick is still there! T was certain it would be. I love that certainty of his, and that of his brother; one can rest in others' certainties sometimes. Next, a bit of shopping .. now each boy has a set of castanets. On the outskirts of town we stop at a wayside church, as I tend to do every day, every time I see one. A fellow there tells the boys about, of all things, castanets! The Andalusians attach castanets to their thumbs, and here in the north, they are attached to the first finger and the middle finger, or to the middle finger only. Much rhythmic happy clacketing ensues.

Totally different landscape. Dry. Scrub. Huge Scotch broom (or its Spanish cousin). We see a snake and different sizes of green lizards. Two are huge. Hot. So hot. We must start early early tomorrow.

We come to Santa Catalina de Somoza .. all walls of stone. An old man just outside of town tells us to go to the second albergue. We check the first, *"Puedo ver..?"* May we look..? It's so clean! And then, we go to the second. It is similar, but all of the rooms are reserved! So, we wander the town to see what else we might find. SO much renovation happening. The whole town is bustling!! We return to the first albergue, check in, do laundry, nap, go to a café for dinner. Watching an episode of a television show, it is dramatically lit like a soap opera. We understand so much, even without full fluency in Spanish.

O Santiago, we are in the river, your river .. this stretch is quieter, or we are quieter .. *Gracias por todos!!*

Four Relinquishments

Relinquishment of self-will
Relinquishment of the feeling of separateness
Relinquishment of attachments
Relinquishment of all negative feelings

Peace Pilgrim

(The 4 Relinquishments are preceded by
the 4 Preparations and the 4 Purifications)

Santa Catalina de Somoza to Rabanal

Wretchedly noisy foursome started messing with their backpacks at 4:30 (plastic is so brutally loud and grating) and they kept at it until 6:00! They awakened everyone, and did not apologize. Sigh. A tad of foresight yesterday, and they would have been ready, or, could have finished their preparations in the foyer. Oh well, we are all awake now.

In glorious contrast, at 6:30, the swallows are in a great uproar, filling the albergue with their conversation about the rain last night, the huge storm front that roared through. It was so excellent to be safe inside, in one's nest, or, in one's bed. Such a clean albergue! The housekeeper has just changed the sheets, and the clean ones have all been ironed!

Then, a flock of folk at breakfast, as twittery and happy as the swallows had been! Many have come up from Madrid. Santa Catalina is so lovely, drystone walls, drystone everything, and seemingly every building being renovated as second homes for *los gatos*, the Madrileños.

Gorgeous overcast morning, the earth and plants smelling so good after their bath last night. Heathers. Slate. Flowers I don't recognize. Walking next to the road. Beautiful high scrub. Steady slope upward, but easy. Granite. Shale. Sandstone. Limestone. Quartz. A metallic teal beetle on a flower. Cuckoos. So many songbirds. Prayers and litanies of gratitude flow easily here ..

Rabanal. Lovely. Stone. Tidy. We go to the albergue recommended to us this morning. Nice family! A darling little dog happily plays with the boys. A Benedictine monk comes to the courtyard/bar for an ice cream. Vespers at 19:00 he tells me. M and T and I go looking for a horseriding place .. walking through roadworks and up to a deserted place .. no people, plenty of horses. Disappointing. Then we stop by the English-run albergue to see their library .. from the *Rubáiyát* by Omar Khayyam (translated by E. Fitzgerald):

Ah, my Beloved,
fill the cup that clears
today of past regrets and future fears.

There is also a 1969 edition of the Guiness Book of World Records which the boys are allowed to borrow and peruse for a few hours. There are so many people in this world, and there is the full spectrum of abilities and gifts. All is well .. Am happy to see Desiderata on the wall here (in Spanish) .. *Go placidly amid the noise and haste ..*

A quick rest, then to the church. Just outside the door, that same monk comes out and asks me if I will read a bit from the Bible that he has marked.. something from Peter. I like the words .. It is an honour. I say yes. He gives the same reading also to a German, a Frenchwoman and a Spaniard. The service is in Latin. Then the reading .. Spanish, German, French. I am shaking .. I want the words to go through everyone, to imbue them with Grace ..

After, at the shop next to the monastery, the boys each choose a small sculpture. Then to the albergue .. *Gracias Santiago por este día maravilloso!*

Die Liebe wirkt magisch.
Sie ist der Endzweck
der Weltgeschichte,
das Amen des Universums.

Love works magic.
She is the final goal
of the world story,
the amen of the universe.

Novalis

Rabanal to Foncebadón

"*Aunque sólo sea en actidud de búsqueda..
devotionis affectu, voti vel pietatis causa..*".. Our new
Credencial de Pelegrino (the first one we each
started out with is full) refers to what is sought
in pilgrimage. Lovely to think about, to practise.
Seeking. Devotion. Prayer.

The noisy pilgrims start early, and lying in my
bunk with my eyes closed, I want to capture the
sound of it, so completely evocative of the typico
albergue/refugio of the Camino .. the plastic
sounds, the zippers, the sliding and dropping
and banging and crunching, the muttering and
chattering, the alarm clocks, all of it. Z (of the
albergue) gives the boys each a coffee cake for
breakfast, and enthusiastic kisses of good will and
good luck. We leave to the waves and smiles of Z
and her extended family.

It is grey out. Low clouds. Beautifully poetic with
the grey stone, the lichen, the small mossy trees,
as T says, "it's mystical .." It is all uphill, but like
yesterday, gentle. The clouds lower around us, that

dreamstate of fog is evoked. A field of unfurling bracken, bright green against the foggy backdrop. Silent. We climb higher. A valley of rock walls and bracken and grass and a quartz fountain! A huge, beautiful stone with water pouring out of it, centered in a rectangular basin. Gorgeous!

Higher still, heather everywhere, purple and white .. and some bracken, and some broom with its vivid yellow. And the rock, is this shale? Lichen-covered, exquisite! The heather reminds me of Cicely Mary Barker's poem so I chant it to the boys ..

The Song of The Heather Fairy

Ho, Heather Ho! From south to north
Spread now your royal purple forth!
Ho, jolly one! From east to west,
The moorland waiteth to be dressed!
I come, I come! With footsteps sure
I run to clothe the waiting moor;
From heath to heath I leap and stride
To fling my bounty far and wide.

We pause amidst this incredible beauty, and the clouds lift! We can see all of the way down the valley to Rabanal! Oh we have loved this walk this morning! Thinking of the Cruz de Ferro, of patterns we each want to be quit of, we find rock volunteers to add to the volunteers we got with E&F. Then, we each focus on a powerful beautiful I AM .. which we each state for ourselves on this glorious hillside. *Gracias Santiago (and the flower fairies!)*

Walking onward, we come to Foncebadón. A dog howling. Ragged. Hmm, maybe we want to forge onward .. but Z warned us away from Monjardin. Hmmm, continue to the Cruz? We find an open albergue run by hippies, which is familiar, but the energy here is strongly dark-light mixed. Some folk, pilgrims? friends? are chanting ohm guru ohm guru and other songs and chants, which is a powerful way of holding space, and again mixed, dark-light. Posted is a Spanish translation of Oriah Mountain Dreamer's beloved poem, which begins ..

> *It doesn't interest me*
> *what you do for a living.*
> *I want to know*
> *what you ache for*
> *and if you dare to dream*
> *of meeting your heart's longing ..*

On the lovely fireplace altar is a card which says: "I am not the same .. having seen the moon shine on the other side of the world." (by Mary Anne Radmacher) One of the chanters is the hospitalera and she shows us a room, and we decide to stay. The boys play happily, chess and checkers, and a Nepalese game called Goats & Tigers, (Bagh-Chal). L, the nine-year-old son of the hospitaleros arrives. How fun! The three boys run around the property having a grand time. L also shows the boys a computer game about ancient Rome.

Then L's dad offers to take all three riding, on a lead rope. It feels okay .. and it is on the boys' list of must-do experiences, and we were just talking about it yesterday. Still, I find myself getting up to go check on them .. I arrive at the field just as M's horse, not on a lead(!), starts bucking!!! He holds on, then somehow pushes himself away, lands and rolls away to safety.

As M said afterward, "I was put on a horse when the nice man said we could go riding, but it was a 'green' horse. Almost everyone, when we are around horses, thinks I have an amazing ability with horses, so he put me on it. Suddenly it started bucking and Mom and T said I stayed on the horse very well. I remember pushing myself away from the horse so I could clear it. It reared up twice and kicked its heels once. I landed, and all that happened was I hurt my knee and T and the man helped me up. Mom said I looked like a stunt rider from the films and T said I was amazing. Then I got on the boy's horse and rode that and everything was great."

Of course I am furious with the dishonest father, and sick that I did not pay closer attention before I said yes. My dear fellow, bruised and shaken, and so brave! It was extraordinary to watch him .. he looked as though he had done this before, riding a bucking bronco! Then, in his brave calm way, he rides L's horse, which is well-trained. What a strange experience; those mixed energies of this place made manifest.

Later, the three boys run out into the huge hail and lightning storm. They make quick dashes outside to feel the hail, to see how far away the lightning is, to count the seconds betwixt light and sound.

Tomorrow, the Iron Cross .. *Dear Santiago, Let me leave all of my burdens there, and all I have carried for others, so that they may be free. Dear God, let me then go forward in some way with Thy blessings unto the World, with Thy Grace, Thy Love, Thy Light ..*

Blessing of the Nine Elements

May you go forth under the strength of heaven,
Under the light of sun,
Under the radiance of moon;
May you go forth with the splendor of fire,
With the speed of lightning,
With the swiftness of wind;
May you go forth supported by the depth of sea,
By the stability of earth,
By the firmness of rock;
May you be surrounded and encircled,
Above, below, and about,
With the protection of the nine elements.

Caitlin Matthews

FONCEBADÓN TO ACEBO TO PONFERRADA

Didn't wake up the boys until after the room was empty of other pilgrims. L appears, eager for their company, and whisks T and M downstairs to continue the computer game about ancient Rome, and they chatter happily. As we are heading out, the man M refers to as "Paolo Coelho's dog" appears in the village. Am grateful we are on the move, away. The Camino is fascinating. Who one sees, and when. Some again, and some not. The mysteries of the River ..

Lowering clouds, so beautiful! The boys and I start up and out through the village. M's knee is hurting terribly and he and T have heavy heavy rocks intended for the Cruz de Ferro. We come to a beautiful location with a cross and a pond .. impeccable! The boys imbue their rocks with all they want to be quit of and heave them into the water. Their faces are glowing when they turn around! Then we begin the climb up to the Cruz de Ferro .. lovely .. heathers .. glimpses of distant valleys .. the clouds around us .. other pilgrims appear and disappear in the fog. I sight the Cruz across the valley from us, hilltop to hilltop. Up and down and around .. then we come toward it .. a huge pile of rocks at the base. Pilgrims climbing and placing things, rocks and notes and photos etc. A parking lot across the street, a seating area on both sides of the street. We wait at the edge of the pine trees for the wave of pilgrims to be complete. Our moment, the three of us placing rocks at different places, with focused intention, good-bye fears, good-bye to all I have carried .. *Thank you Cruz de Ferro for transforming all into nameless and formless energy!*

We continue, stopping for 10 seconds in Monjardin, yikes. *Bless you Z for your direction!* We walk on .. I keep hearing, *I am free in name and form and deed and eternity. I am free and you are free.* Rocky pathways. Rain coming. We get our raingear on just in time. The boys are planning the next 10 years of their lives, full of the vitality of Life. The rain becomes torrential. Steep hills, the downhills very rocky and slippery. Knees hurt. (Drat L's dad! Darn darn darn! Generally and specifically.)

We come to Acebo. Ancient village. Small balconies of dark wood overhanging the single street with its central water channel, which is full of rushing water. We follow signs for the mercado and step out of the rain, through the hanging screen, to the sweet kind faces of a darling darling elder couple. When she asks how I am, I say that our knees hurt, so she insists that her husband call for a taxi to Ponferrada (!) .. and then she makes us the most delicious hot omelette sandwiches. Further, they gift us each with a beautiful apple. The taxi arrives and the driver visits with the couple while we eat. Then the elder gentleman goes outside into the rain as we say our fare thee wells to his sweet generous wife. How did he know they were there, the sheep? He waves the herd away! The taxi motors slowly and carefully through the plaza .. then zoom! We go! *Ultreia!* Whooshing past pretty villages .. into Ponferrada, a huge albergue. A room for 4 for us, the Virgen de La Encina room, the hospitalero tells us .. The Virgin of the Evergreen Oak ..

We scout Ponferrada. Looking at the 12th century Templar castle, the boys insist we explore it tomorrow. This is rather a ghastly city. Gang scrawls everywhere, so sad. Everything is closed too, shops, restaurants. Maybe it's a Monday thing.

Back at the albergue .. must heal our knees! I massage our wonder-full unguent into our knees, especially M's. Boys online researching ancient

Rome and Ancient Greece. Very much wanting to custom-design gear for the next walk.

This, on a wall: *El Camino es tiempo de meditació interior, no intenerario turístico.* (The Camino is a time of interior meditation, not a tourist itinerary.)

Gracias Santiago por la Cruz de Ferro! O Santiago, bendice el tipo pareja de anciano de Acebo!

*It is very useful to travel on land and sea
to places where the intellect is illuminated,
the love of God is stimulated,
life transformed into a better state,
one's own merits increased,
And the experience of useful things acquired.*

Felix Fabri
15th C.

PONFERRADA TO CACABELOS

We awaken .. wait .. for something (?) then fall back to sleep .. to be awakened later by the kind hospitalero, checking on our safety. (Ah, there was a fight earlier, apparently. Am so grateful the boys didn't have to witness that!) Onward! We know we want to see the castle, but maybe we can find a café open today? We walk along the main street, which feels markedly safer than the waymarked Camino alley. Yes! Across the street from the castle, a lovely amusing designer-y café, with Phillipe Starck chairs and many beautiful elegant details. Delicious croissants made on site. Delicious everything! Well, we stay here for two hours!

Up to the castle. 11:00. Across the drawbridge. They stamp our credenciales and kindly let us leave our backpacks behind the ticket kiosk. We are curious about Paolo's account. Of course, he was here, having his Templar-ish experience, long before the castle was renovated. From the outside, Ponferrada castle looks solid, but once inside, it reveals itself to be only three walls, with ruins in the middle. Though evocative, we are still disappointed. Supposedly this was originally the largest Templar castle in Spain. Shaped roughly in a pentagon, with twelve towers linked to the zodiac, and, to the Freemasons. Perhaps it was, and is, linked with the stars, with the Way of Stars, but it does not reveal its secrets to us this Tuesday in April. The boys run about and explore for an hour. Then we return again to the beautiful café for a delicious lunch.

We walk out of town, but it's so awful, dirty, dusty, angry, despairing. This brings up an intense quit-the-Camino energy in all of us, so, I shift us all by flagging a taxi. Whoosh to Cacabelos! We come to an albergue in the churchyard, little rooms of two beds each. It is filthy, but it is all that is available. That enough-of-this snarly feeling returns, offset, fortunately, for the boys, by a charming sixteen-year-old German boy who is also staying at the albergue. I give him one of the mementos from Notre-Dame. This is a Strange Road day, and thank God tomorrow will come. I think of the ancient Egyptians, so grateful to see the sun each morning. I hold that promise of Light as I go to sleep. *Buenos noches Santiago.*

*Do not seek
to follow in the footsteps
of the wise,
seek what they sought.*

Matsuo Basho

CACABELOS TO VILLAFRANCA DEL BIERZO

Out the door .. vaguely following a lovely (physically and in manners) Brazilian couple and their friends. An elder, with his cane, speeds past us and directs them along the road. Perhaps he is their guardian angel? *Peace Love Peace Love* The boys are bubbling over with game ideas and inventions. At the crest of a hill, we follow the painted arrows into the vineyards .. and oh oh oh, my cup of happiness everfloweth. The vineyards here in Bierzo are not only in leaf but have baby grapes. In this gorgeous valley, amid the vine rows there are cherry trees, some with almost-ripe cherries. We pass a huge, ancient, tree, each branch propped up by cut branches of some other tree. We come through the vineyards to the old old village of Villatuilla Arriba. Perhaps medieval pilgrims passed though here. On the right, café tables?! Oh such luck! An old man has converted his garage into a café! He is seated with a map of Europe behind him and a telephone and a book next to him. He shows us old black and white photos of himself, so long he has lived here, on the Camino. We are so happy to pause and have breakfast, just the three of us sharing this beautiful morning with this dear elder who so loves the Camino.

We continue onward, so happy! Along Calle de Camino de Santiago. The houses look medieval. How is it to live in them now? Very deeply, this is a place from another era. I notice litre water bottles full of water spaced along the ground next to the wall of one building .. why? The village ends, and we are back on the dirt track. Again, so pleasing! Swallows swooping and darting. Small gardens next to some of the vineyards. Vines and roses. Some German teenagers come striding up. A moment of hellos betwixt all of the boys. Will M & T walk the Camino again when they are 17 (as these charming fellows are now) they wonder? A photo must be taken, smiles abound. *May their two weeks resonate beautifully in their hearts, in their souls.* I realize these teens are the first Germans I have spoken with who are making a religious journey, a pilgrimage. Their 'Buen caminos' fade as their long long legs take them into their future(s).

Fennel lines the path. Cuckoos (but probably doves) in the distance. Songbirds as happy as we are. We come to Villafranca del Bierzo .. so lovely, on the hillside, and below and across the little valley. We are so happy today. The walk was so lovely. The 12th century Church of Santiago is on our left. We walk around the back to the door on the western side. Inside is stark, austere. A man in charge of photos and sellos (stamps for the credenciales) sits at a table in the stillness. I ask if the closed and barred doors we saw outside are the Puerta del Perdón. The man says indeed, and that they are only open during the Santiago holy years and on his feast day, July 25th. Ah, well, we are going all of the way to Santiago, so we walk through the Puerta del Perdón doorway simply by placing our hands on either side of the door and matching our hands just so, all the while intending that we are passing though. Pardons asked for, pardons given. We then sit outside on the doorsill of the Puerta, our backs to the great door itself, and I read to the boys about Paolo's travels from Villafranca to O Cebreiro.

Suddenly, the man from the church is standing in front of us! "Come here, I will explain something to you", he says. So we step down from the doors and this lovely generous man explains them to us! (In Spanish) "Above the arch shows scenes from Santiago's life. The five columns on each side are like hands, the five fingers. The door points to the north and to the Camino saluting each pilgrim who passes. Facing the doors, on the left, the Colosseum in Rome, and the crucifixion and see the three Magi and the three muertos and the angel .. and the adoration of the Virgin, see with baby Jesus on her knee. On the right, fruit, vines, mythic animals, griffins, vines." What a gift!! He smiles and then carefully takes out of his billfold a ten euro note and pointing, shows us that here, on the note, is the Puerta del Perdón! This had been affirmed by an official. And then he carefully and reverently puts the note away. We thank him profusely for his *amabilidad* and continue on our way with last waves good bye to him, and to the patient patient doors.

Straight ahead is a castle! Oh it's beautiful! The woman selling cherries on the corner tells us it belongs to the Marquis, that it's private, since the 1600s. How marvelous! Down through the town. Narrow, winding streets. Beautiful photography in one shop. Onward through the Plaza Mayor, feeling our way. Ah, this albergue! A charming young couple have built this place, this refuge. Clean sheets! (fourth time in 39 days, not that we're counting). Toilet paper! Soap! We ask to stay for two nights as it is so very pleasing to all of us. They have a great dog. We are so happy to be here.

Later, to the Iglesia de San Francisco. They say St. Francis himself founded it. A sweet elder therein provides a sello for our credenciales. I light a candle of thanks to Santiago. It makes me feel like weeping. The elder man is so sweet. Here, high on the hill, a sweeping view of the town, slate roofs, the castle, the far hills.

Into the Plaza Mayor, bustling cafés, happy people. We explore, finding magnifying lenses, and a mini chess set. Beautifully crafted small folding knives, from a shop that has been there for decades. Also, a handsome sweater T wants for his teenage self. Then at the albergue, we receive the blessing of foot massages and reiki from a wonderful healer. She channels, "seeing" for each of us. When she massages my feet, I can literally feel the resolution and completion of so much. This is as a birth-day for me. It feels as if my feet are being pardoned! We are all three transformed by her care!

Today we ask for more time.. Fifteen more days? Thirty? Forty?

O Santiago, bless the elder man of the café in Villatuilla, with his dreams of the Camino, and bless the kind man from your church in Villafranca who told us about your doors. Please bless the elder of the Iglesia de San Francisco. And Santiago, the lovely couple of our albergue, their beautiful dog, and the lady healer – please bless them. Thank you Santiago for your beautiful Camino of kindnesses and generosity!

On Life's journey
faith is nourishment,
virtuous deeds are a shelter,
wisdom is the light by day
and right mindfulness
is the protection by night.
If a man lives a pure life,
nothing can destroy him.

Buddha

Villafranca del Bierzo

Rest day. Assimilation. We go the correos twice. We are given the same room in the albergue as yesterday. The dog has adopted the boys. We write in our journals and the boys experiment with their magnifying glasses. They also stroll down to the river and try to catch lizards .. much chasing and laughing, mixed with their river of ideas .. so many ideas for inventions, games, and more!

We see the lady healer again. She shares with me the meanings of places. Bierzo is feelings/ water. Galicia is air/thoughts. She speaks also of Santiago and of Finisterre. As I listen, I feel so strongly, *Now I am in my new life of happiness.* My feet are new. I am not the same person as yesterday. She gives the boys Reiki. *Gracias Santiago for your history, your mystery, the blessings we receive in many forms!*

Life is an opportunity,
benefit from it.
Life is beauty,
admire it.
Life is a dream,
realize it.
Life is an adventure,
dare it.
Life is luck,
make it.
Life is a promise,
fulfill it.

Mother Teresa

VILLAFRANCA TO VEGA DE VALCARCE

Hard to leave our true refuge. The owners and their dog got up early to have breakfast with us. At 7:30 we are out the door, and along the road. Along the road all day .. *Peace Love Peace Love* .. Hard cement underfoot, but the river is below us.. So many plants! Yarrow. Fennel, which I put under my backpack straps, the smell is so pleasing. Cherry trees. Wild roses. Purple clover. Cottonwood. Hollyhock. Wild strawberries. Brambles. Red oriental poppies. Huge hazelnut trees. Trees with their feet in the cool river.

As the morning goes on, more and more traffic. Huge trucks, one carrying a 50 or 60 foot cement beam, perhaps for a bridge? We are nine kilometres from the political border of Galicia, but the land doesn't know that and is already shifting. We talk about places we have loved along the Camino. Off the road .. a shady walk into Trabadelo. A huge huge chestnut tree. First albergue is so creepy, we cannot leave fast enough! Then, a kilometre later, a lovely bar run by a lovely woman. Fair Trade coffee for the first time on the Camino. A funny cat who adores the boys. Delicious sandwiches, cream cheese with fines herbes on great bread. Continue into the furnace of the day. Stop in another village for a drink and a pin for each of the boys. I carry a small compass in my pouch of prayers .. and some dirt from the Santuario de Chimayo, and a khata from a gathering with HH the Dalai Lama, and there is a quartz crystal, and some small scallop shells. It is a pouch of deep devotion, of many aspects of the Divine Mystery. One of the prayers is for Light, calling to the Sun .. *Please, let me be of Light rather than darkness, of Love rather than fear.* Taking out the compass, I think about my own seeking for direction .. seeking the Sacred, its timelessness, the holographic sensation of that ..

Vega de Valcarce. The albergue, refugio, up the hill to the right. No one there, but a sign telling everyone to pick their beds. Empty cool room. Blazing hot outside. I do our laundry. The boys meet two huge green lizards. We go foraging for dinner. Nothing. Thank god for our delicious lunch! Then the hospitalero makes bocadillos for us. Blessed be!

When I close my eyes, I can feel the ground underfoot, the sense of each stride, each footfall, specific moments of today, bright with sunshine and clarity. *Thank you Santiago! Good night Camino, good night to all who wander, to all who seek, to all who are found.*

Be like the honeybee
Who gathers only nectar
Wherever it goes.
Seek the goodness
That is found in everyone.

Amma
(Mata Amritanandamayi Deva)

Vega de Valcarce to O Cebreiro

I slept so very well, awakening from a prophetic dream. I change the pin on my shirt. Today, the chalice. I am so grateful for how cool it is this morning. We are out the door very early. The boys tell me a wonderful thing: after I fell asleep last night, they went outside and the lady hospitalero saw them and made them nutella sandwiches and bought them candy! All of which they have saved to share with me, the darlings! So we share the sandwiches for breakfast as we walk. Such a blessing because nothing is open. At a private hotel overlooking the valley in Herrerias, a fellow is setting up breakfast for his guests and kindly gives us colacao and coffee and a plate of cookies. Such a lovely pause. Who knows when we will come upon such a pretty place again. *Santiago, please thank him from us!* Onward .. *left right* .. through the valley .. then up. Today we have crossed the threshold into Galicia. The wind happily greets us, taking some of the bite out of the fierce heat. We climb up and up from the Valcarce valley floor.. past chestnut trees and grazing dairy cows. We share the narrow trail for a bit with four huge brown cows, their bells clanging, their soft brown eyes so contemplative and sweet. Wanting to stop, we have to keep walking, in part because there is nowhere we could stop to sleep, and in part because we kept thinking of O Cebreiro, curious. Thus we are pulled upward and upward. Every time I think we have come to the top, another hillside beckons, and the valley slowly recedes into a purple distance.

So, six hours of walking, four of them up up up .. partly with wonderful stone underfoot .. trying to remember if the Romans built a road through here. Then along a long high stone wall providing blessed shade on our right, some other valley far below us to the left .. *Peace Love* .. we come up and out, and it's O Cebreiro! Grey stone everything. Two tour buses, scads of people. Oh well. Find the albergue. New. Modern lines. Huge room with high ceilings and 56 people for company! A magnificent westward view into another valley .. we are so high!

This is an old place, this O Cebreiro. The church of Santa Maria la Real was begun in the 9th century and blessed by a miracle of the chalice and paten hundreds of years ago. Queen Isabella stayed in O Cebreiro during her pilgrimage to Santiago in 1486. The people speak Spanish and

Gallegos, a Gaelic variant. The two shops sell Celtic jewelry, and lots of things with witches on them, and aprons with different soup recipes on them, and walking sticks, and scallop shells made of everything you can imagine. Exploring the village, we see several restored *pallozas* of three rooms: one for the head of the household, one for animals, one for everything (everyone?) else. They are of stone walls, circular or oval, with a thatched pointed conical roof. They date from Celtic times, not these same buildings per se, but the design is more than 1500 years old. We saw a 'real' one, as in still lived in, as we were climbing earlier today. I want to visit the church after the tourists leave. A nap for the boys while I write this. All of the time we have been here, I keep thinking of Dorothy looking around Oz and saying, "we're not in Kansas anymore".. this, O Cebreiro. There is much much more here than meets the eye. Words like 'liminal' and 'evanescent' and 'other-worldly' brush the mind ..

I do go into the church. For all that it was entirely rebuilt in the 1960s, it is redolent of history, time out of time. Here, it is easy to see why religions build upon earlier sacred sites .. *the Sacred comes through.* It is quiet. Still. And full .. of miracles. Shhhhhh .. *Gracias Santiago! Gracias Maria!*

Divinity is
In its onmniscience
And omnipotence
Like a wheel,
A circle,
A whole,
That neither be understood,
Nor divided,
Nor begun,
Nor ended.

Hildegard of Bingen

O CEBREIRO TO FONFRÍA

We read the last chapter of *The Pilgrimage*, a bit disgusted with Paolo's whining, and the fact that he ducks out from O Cebreiro to Santiago. However, as is said, his path. We are happy we still have Marcus Aurelius and Zen as companions.

I have received an important email, and keep turning it over and over .. "the new hierarchy of Man".. hmmm. I wonder .. *Is one more important for who one was in another lifetime? Does that influence this life truly? If we didn't know what we know, would we each be more or less than who we are now?* Good contemplation material, to walk with above the metronome of *Peace Love Peace Love*.

We walk downhill and uphill and downhill. Many many beautiful butterflies! All different colours. Delightful! At the edge of a village, a dog comes up to the boys and wants to be petted, then smiles and leans against T's legs.

We pass an albergue which looks to be in a pig sty. Will wonders never cease?!

Three kilometres on, we come to this albergue – which has the best library ever!

A book on plants .. a Latin and Spanish litany of beauty .. I read them aloud .. *Acónito, Berros, Caléndula, Cerezo, Ciruelo, Espliego, Fresa, Hysopo, Olivo* .. on and on .. maravilloso!! Then I find a book on the three Holy Routes: to Santiago, to Rome, to Jerusalem. Other books, replete with fascinating essays, in Latin, Spanish, German and French .. An essay about how King Robert of Scotland asked William of Douglas to carry his heart to Jerusalem after he died!! A beautiful essay about Jesus as a pilgrim. It is such a joy to be able to spend hours poring over these books, these essays. I am grateful beyond words. *Gracias Santiago!*

I enter the temple,
Seek the dream world of monks,
Thumb through the sutras,
Feel the dustiness of this traveler's life.

.

Yuan Hung-Tao
16th C.

FONFRÍA TO TRIACASTELA

I awaken panicked, and open my eyes to a film crew stealthily filming everyone asleep! I loudly tell them to go away! I ask for film releases and business cards which slows them down and helps the other awakening pilgrims to tell them to stop. How invasive and disrespectful! Such beastly entitlement! (As for the other layer of panic, I learn about the plane crash later .. ah, my sorrow for all .. those as they left this life so suddenly, those left behind to mourn them ..)

After the camera crew leaves, I get the boys up and we gather our wits and pack up. Then, a café con leche for me, and colacao for the boys. Out into the village. By the last house an old woman is standing in the path .. with a plate of crêpes covered by a cloth, and a shaker jar of sugar. In ten seconds we are each holding one, befuddled at her determination and at her refusal to accept our "no gracias". Thinking this is another instance of someone gifting the boys with a sweet, we smile, and then her eyes quickly calculate .. "Un euro. Uno, uno, uno," she says, pointing at each of us .. oof! Ah well, she needs it, and made the effort, this good food .. so there it is. *Bendice en su cocina, dear lady.*

Then onward .. through another beautiful morning. Hot sun, breeze, and our kilometres today are often in the shade. Paths edged with drystacked stone walls. After last night's book of plants, those we pass are now faces with names, as it were, and it feels so friendly to know their names. As I look at the angelica, I remember reading that, in days of yore, poets would make crowns of it to wear for inspiration!

M and T run ahead and take off their packs, then sit under a tree. They look *radiant* when I come to them, radiant! *The sight of awakened wonder .. the glow of happiness, of feeling the joy of a place, of the moment of connection, the expansion of the heart that follows instantaneously ..*

As I walk along .. *Peace Love Peace Love* .. admiring the long vistas into small valleys, watching the boys dash and leap and walk and rest .. am thinking about some fascinating essays I read last night about medieval pilgrims. There have always been the tourists. There have always been those who made a vow. And those who experience a vision. There have always been those hoping for a miracle. And those collecting indulgences, (the get-out-of-hell passes). There has always been the debate betwixt those who believe they are closer to God by staying home and living as religiously or spiritually as they can ("life-pilgrimage") and those who believe there is greater merit in journeying to holy sites ("place-pilgrimage"). There have always been egoic arguments as to the relative holiness of one's approach to the pilgrimage itself. For example, holiness accrued via prayers per guidebooks, yes, hundreds of years ago, there were guidebooks indicating which churches to visit and which statues or paintings to pray to. This, versus holiness accrued via making it alive to the end, to the holy destination, and back home to tell the tale. It makes me think of *A Distant Mirror*, Barbara Tuchman's brilliant book about the 14th century. Oh, the parallels, then to now!

My musings are interrupted by a woman, a pilgrim with a walking stick adorned by a cross, and, in her other hand, a plastic bag full of cherries. She insists upon giving scrumptious handfuls to the boys .. such a lovely gesture! Two happy boys .. and thus we come to Triacastela. Dirt streets and a big road project beginning at the far end of town. We look at three albergues .. and choose the third one, with the monks' vestments hanging on the wall in all their gilt-embroidered intricacy. Tomorrow,

Samos monastery .. I hope it is both what, and where, I am seeking.

I have a moment of the many faces of the kind folk we have met on the Camino flashing before me .. *Are they all the faces of God? Indeed. Gracias a Dios y Santiago por sus amabilidad!*

.. On the Camino you need ..
To believe that humans have more virtues than
vices. To accept that those mistakes we make
along the way are only signs of our humanity. To
carry on along the road, although at times you
fall; for by rising up you learn. To believe through
love, and not from fear; if you have fear, you may
fear to love. To believe freely. Faith is not a bur-
den. Not to be a slave, except to Love.
If you sense Love,
you will sense it is all around you.

Augusto Losada López
Parish Priest of Triacastela

The Camino de Santiago: The Human and Spiritual
Dimension

Triacastela to Samos

We woke up so happy! Last folk to leave the albergue .. which gives the Dutch hospitalero enough time to spend a moment in fare thee wells with us .. then off we go .. along the road. A hot day. We are happy! "Happiness is a mystery, like religion, and should never be rationalized." (G.K. Chesterton) There you have it .. so, we are mysteriously gratefully happy. A pause at a roadside waterfall, the boys drawing. I add a chalk labyrinth to the scene, knowing it will be washed away by the rain in a few days. Then, the Way diverges from the road and we are on soft loam under the green shade of huge old oak trees and maples. A stream below us. Small plots of farmland. Haying. Then an absolutely empty village .. like a set for another time, a bit eerie. I photograph the shadow of the church tower .. it makes more sense than the church itself.

On the far side of the village, one old man, his gnarled hands holding a bucket with a bright green lettuce in it. Onto the old quiet loamy path again. Old stone walls. A small church, locked.

We peer through the keyhole to greet Mary standing quietly there.

We are happily by ourselves, only a few other pilgrims today. T says he feels "Santiago and the monastery pulling us." He and M are joyfully overflowing with ideas. *Peace Love .. Joy Joy .. Peace Love .. Joy Joy ..* An old mill, the water rushing under it. A sign or declaration with a family name faded by time. Beginning to think Samos doesn't exist, we climb a hill, go through an underpass and find a sign for it! Another half kilometre. Thank goodness for the shade! Then, there it is! Down in the valley to the right. Two cloisters .. the main presence of the village. As we descend, there is a very high stone wall with regular tower/buttresses along it, green with moss and climbing plants, alas, completely blocking my view down to the monastery. Then, two hairpin turns, and we are in the village, looking across the river. The monastery as backdrop. In the middle, two monks are hoeing the many-acre garden. In the foreground, a grey donkey and two longhorned red cattle and three geese. I scan my memories of paintings, for surely this is reminiscent of one .. a Book of Hours ..

We walk around to the front entrance to the church, a grand staircase, and to the right of it, a monk standing in another doorway. Ah, he tells us, the albergue is further around, and, it doesn't open until 15:00. Mass is at 19:30. Right, to lunch then, at the café we glimpsed when we initially sighted Samos from above! It faces the albergue door. By 14:30 there is a line of *mochillas* (backpacks) along the wall. Several monks appear, black briefcases matching their black robes, and enter a different door. Finally, we check in and choose our beds .. not so clean .. but with paintings on the walls inspired by illuminated manuscripts.

M finds out that by standing on a certain top bunk, he can see into the cloister. His relentless curiosity is a delight! A few moments later, as we step back outside to the street, a German man and his fourteen-year-old son arrive on bicycles. I help translate. They wish to camp .. yes .. across and up, by the chapel just beyond the stone wall. All three boys are happy about this. We pause for a bit to give time for camp setup, then go over. Just beyond them is a lovely park and a wide cool river. Stone walls, meandering paths, bridges with iron scallop shell designs. Of course all three boys end up playing and swimming in the river! There are blue dragonflies darting about .. the symbols of change and Light.

An hour later, I have to see the monastery.

M and T join me on the tour of the cloisters and the church. There is one old part left, a doorway with an interesting symbol carved in the stone above .. a combination of the Templar cross and infinity symbols, our guide says. The lovely cloister gardens, an elder monk tending to the larger one. Oh, so wonderful! High walls, plants and a fountain inside .. wide wide porticoed passageways, the cloisters .. to pace .. contemplating .. contemplating. Then, upstairs, the (54 metre) long walls have been painted with a dramatic (melodramatic? florid? certainly larger than life) sequence of St. Benedict's life. My favourite part shows him writing his rules, with his friend and confidante – a raven! – at his feet. The sad part is that the monastery, a thousand years old then, burned down in 1951, leaving the stone skeleton. There is a stark series of black and white photos. So, thence into their church .. with those photos in mind, one wonders where the current statues came from. Back downstairs to the cloisters, sunlight patterning the black and white stone.

As we leave the cool building, stepping out into the bright heat, the boys almost catch a lizard. Still seeking .. something .. the boys and I walk back to the albergue. The hospitalero is a monk, who looks at us and gestures to us. Discreetly ..

we follow him across and up to the tiny hermitage chapel. He points out the cypress towering over us. It too is a thousand years old. Imagining being inside the chapel .. *the stillness, the presence of the elder cypress, the quality of Grace .. a sigh, a prayer .. heartfelt thanks for this moment .. in this there is every thing, every where, every when .. sigh .. so deep the peace ..*

Like poetry,
Pilgrimage is beyond time and space.
It happens now,
Or it doesn't happen at all.

Phil Cousineau

SAMOS TO SARRIA

Suddenly we are aware of the hours of the day, the days of the week, the days of the month .. and how little time we seemingly have left. Not wanting this to end, and, equally desperate for hours and days of uninterrupted sleep .. the boys have begun talking about home and that familiar life. Thus, our attention is split. We talk about earlier days and moments on the Camino and our excitement and curiosity then, and what it feels like now ..

Leaving the albergue, the monastery, a last long look back. At the end of the village, bronze statues of pilgrims, all in medieval garb. He is ahead cresting a stone rise, facing west. She is (in her long skirt, like me) facing back toward her son. He has the short cape with scallops that we saw at the Hermitage de St Nicholas. He is standing at the fountain .. ah yes, playing with water! The boys are most pleased with the "niño" and pose for a moment. Onward. It is overcast, lovely respite from the heat! Walking along the road, past a seating area built to showcase the stone workers' skills, with signs explaining same. The river is close ..

Oh! wide stepping stones. Two boys happily bound across! A small village, Teixos, across the highway has a small tidy church. I cross whilst the boys head for the waterfall on the river. Peering in the window .. it's Santiago! Hola! Hello! How marvelous!

We carry on, past farmland, pasturage. We come past a pretty courtyard with purple rhododendrons .. and there is a small shrine, the stone statue worn .. we can see the prayerful hands still. Then, groves of young poplars, so lovely in the grey mist. It's a dreaming energy, thoughts about how people change .. and how they don't. How we have and haven't. Further along, I realize that while Galicia this far has nothing in common with Ireland except lots of stone walls and buildings .. this landscape, with its density of green shrubbery, reminds me of northern California on the coast. Oh yes, must remember this: slate roofs here of varying sizes .. the ridgeline akin to dragon spines. They use slate for so much here, walls tiled with it, roofs, walls of thick slabs of it, signs. I love how it looks when it is covered with mosses and lichens. The other Galician elements are poverty and dairy cows .. and, oof! .. whatever the cows here eat makes for ghastly smelling manure! I remember clean cows in Switzerland, but these, are not. Sweet faces though. We thank them for their milk and cheese and ice cream! As we continue our rural Way, we notice how few pilgrims we see. Love that! The boys burble on happily .. discussing tinkering and game design and flying and parachuting and sub-atomic space. We pass through a two-building village. One is the church, locked. Peering inside, we see three different statues of Mary waiting quietly through time. I think about how She, in her lovingkindness, holds all children.

A while later .. a tiny elder woman scything the grass in front of her house. Later, a barn with tobacco hanging to dry. The path is lined with grasses taller than the boys! Then, in the sky, a stork .. the first I've seen in days, I realize. We come to Sarria. City outskirts .. and, unloading at the first albergue, that darn film crew! Boundaries boundaries! Up a long wide worn flight of stairs into the old town. It is oddly exhausting to climb. Find an albergue, check in. Crowded beds. Dirty. So we wander in the old town. Not happy with the albergue; some sick people in it (so rare). We find another and are given a private room!! Much better, just what we need. The boys and I gratefully send prayers of thanks to Santiago! *Muchos miles de gracias Santiago!!* Of course I must go into the church .. an iglesia de Maria. *Thank you Mary, thank you!* Chandeliers hanging .. lovely lovely .. the feeling of blessings ..

I am being driven forward
Into an unknown land.
The pass grows steeper,
The air colder and sharper.
A wind from my unknown goal
Stirs the strings
Of expectation.
Still the question:
Shall I ever get there?
There where life resounds,
A clear pure note
In the silence.

Dag Hammarskjöld

SARRIA TO MERCADOIRO

Overcast. Slow to leave. The terrier belonging to the albergue happily trots along with us for a bit, though not long enough for the boys. Past the 13ᵗʰ century Magdalene monastery. Downhill, then across some railroad tracks. A winding path of soft dirt between fields, then up and up. Huge oaks. Green air. Mossy rocks. We are walking so slowly .. it feels as if we are pushing through water .. heavy skies.

I see a church .. Iglesia de Santiago .. an old man in a car out front. As we approach, he carefully gets out, with the key in hand, and silently opens the church for us! A red candle for Santiago .. it will glimmer here for days and days. As we leave, the man .. the priest?.. does too. He locks the church, climbs in his car, and drives away! As if he had been waiting for us?! *O Santiago, thank you for your blessings.*

We continue onward sooooo slowly. A casa rural has a sign with the magic word, café. Yes they do have coffee, and colacao too. It has taken us three hours to walk five kilometres. Good grief! So we pause. The boys swing on the swings in the yard for an hour. I drink coffee until I feel like I can push onward. Such a blessing to have been able to pause here. Then pushing pushing onward.. this strange heavy feeling. Is it the weather changing? I try to distract myself by thinking about rocks .. fences, drystack walls, or rows of slabs three feet high .. or the fence of wooden sticks and barbed wire. It rains for awhile, ever so gently. *Peace Love Peace Love* .. We come upon a meadow of cows and calves. Then two mares and foals, one still wobbly-legged. There are strange granaries, funereal to me .. tall, three or four feet off of the ground. They are similarly sized, on plinths maybe three feet wide, and about six feet tall and twelve long. Many have stone finials at each end. Sides of wood or of small holed ceramic. They remind me of something I saw in Rome .. as I said, funereal.

Past cornfields, young corn. One with last year's withered stalks and overgrown green grass, a testament to a farmer who has left this land and this life. It's so hard to work the land .. elders permanently bent from decades of hoeing. Here, the weeds grow quickly .. a certain wildness hovers at the edges of the tilled fields. In addition, the dairy cattle have to be milked twice a day.

No wonder the young people have fled for the cities .. I wonder which generation has the best quality of life.

We look at the dark rooms of a *casa rural* and pass (on the price as well). Then walk to the next village. The albergue is full. An offer to sleep on the filthy(!) floor of the bar down the hill. No. Onward! We are not feeling terribly tired, well .. we are not thinking about it, so onward. Another four kilometres. A fascinating stretch of rectangular stepping stones, maybe half a kilometre of them, down the center of the lane .. water running down on either side .. granite and sand. There is mica in the rock, glinting, reminding me of the stars. It feels like twilight, but it has felt that way for hours now. A strange day. We are prepared to walk to Portomarin, and then we come around the corner to this property with an albergue. Excellent! Two fellows spent four years restoring and renovating a farmstead .. great design .. so comfortable and peaceful. Lovely view across the valley. Clean. Pleasant café/bar. Nice fellows. Happy other pilgrims. Lucky lucky us! Long hot showers. *Thank you Santiago for bringing us here .. to sleep and sleep well.* It is raining again. Wonderful to be inside and warm and dry!

Whatever the world may say or do,
my part is keep myself good;
just as a gold piece,
or an emerald,
or a purple robe insists perpetually,
'Whatever the world may say or do,
my part is to remain an emerald
and keep my colour true.'

Marcus Aurelius
Book VII. 15

MERCADOIRO

There is something I am neither hearing nor seeing here. It was so close on the meseta and around the hermitage of St. Nicolas .. and in other exquisite moments and places, but here .. nothing. All three of us are sad and out of sorts. The last few days we were so happy, why this change? We feel far away from the heart of this Journey .. in a tunnel almost .. falling toward Santiago.

We decide to stay here in this pretty albergue for another day. The boys chase grasshoppers. It pours rain. We do laundry, we contemplate the imminent end of our glorious journey, we try to distract ourselves. Ooof.

In Spanish, from the simpatico fellow here, "From here to Santiago is three, four maybe five days. Then there is the weather and the money. If it rains, fewer people. If it will be bad weather at the end of the week, fewer people. At the end of the month, fewer people, because of the thinner wallets. People watch the weather thinking, 'It's Thursday, I can make it and still fly home to my country on Monday.' But if it's raining, they won't come. For us with a small albergue, it's good. For the hotels and the big albergues with one hundred beds, it's bad, a day like this, empty, no one. And today is a feast day in Santiago so many people came to be there today. *Buon feria hoy.*"

Torrential icy rains .. asking Santiago to move it all east! Well, change is constant here, so I have that to look forward to. Tomorrow is another day.

Learn the backward step
That turns your light inward
To illuminate your self.

Dogen
13th C.

MERCADOIRO TO GONZAR

Overcast. Lovely. Fresh. T and I are exhausted. M says, *"Santiago is pulling me forward!"* We walk .. to Portomarin .. ghastly place. Thank you Santiago for Mercadoiro! We get rain ponchos .. flimsy, but fun, and, effective. Noisy too we learn .. still, we are drier than we would be. My heels and legs feel like knives, am in agony .. why? Ages later we arrive in Gonzar. A nice albergue, nice family. I rest. The boys play with the children of the albergue owners. *Dear Santiago, can you explain what is going on with me, with us?*

What is the difference
between your experience of existence
and that of a saint?
The saint knows
that the spiritual path
is a sublime chess game with God
and that the Beloved
has just made such a fantastic move
that the saint is now continually
tripping over Joy
and bursting out in Laughter
and saying, "I surrender!"
Whereas, my dear,
I am afraid you still think
you have a thousand serious moves.

Hafiz of Persia

GONZAR TO PALAS DE REY

Overcast. Gentle mist. Thank you Santiago! I wish I liked the landscape more. *Is it my own dearth of positivity that is being reflected?* Hard to be at peace, to proffer peace. The Camino is packed today. Albergues are closed. The one we had hoped to stay in, closed. I wish I was as at ease and curious as the boys are! An area of restored fincas and casas and rural hotels .. all closed. *Is everyone overwhelmed? The roaring rushing tide of pilgrims? Out of sync with the River? And yet, the River is all there is.* Everything smells like manure.

We end up, after 18 kilometres, in Palas de Rey. A rather awful albergue tonight. I had called ahead, based on our wretched erroneous guidebook. We have long since learned not to refer to it, and have thrown most of it away in disgust .. but earlier today I looked at the few pages I had thought to keep .. alas, we did not discern in person, for ourselves. I let fear win today. Oof! The fear of not having a place to sleep .. yet all the while we have had a place to sleep .. every night so far! Still, *Santiago, thank you for the shelter over our heads,* as it is raining. Only solution is to go to bed and get up early and get out of here. Worst snorers of the entire Camino, and, drunk. Aaarrrggh!

This is the way of peace:
Overcome evil with good,
Falsehood with truth,
And hatred with love.

The Golden Rule would do as well. Please don't say lightly that these are just religious concepts and not practical. These are laws governing human conduct, which apply as rigidly as the law of gravity. When we disregard these laws in any walk of life, chaos results. Through obedience to these laws this frightened, war-weary world of ours could enter into a period of peace and richness beyond our fondest dreams.

Peace Pilgrim

Palas de Rey to Melide

Pouring rain. Granted, the first half hour was just overcast. Even in the rain we can see that San Xulian do Camino is a pretty village, the albergue welcoming, but we must forge onward. Then a woodland, offering a bit of shelter from the rain as we walk under the trees. A series of rivers and rivulets to walk through. Feet soaked, icy cold. The signature Galician smell of cow manure is oppressive. As T says, "separating the wheat from the chaff." We come upon a symbol from the ancients. *Thank you!* It is raining in literal sheets, cannot imagine it is possible for more rain to come out of the sky. A bar! Mobbed. A lovely hotel across the way with room for us to pause! Yay! I get newspapers to stuff into our soaking shoes. *Gracias Santiago!* (There weren't any to be found by the time we left.) We wish we were walking through this landscape in non-rain .. as it must be gorgeous. One village has a small strange wattle structure, for grain? In another village, we step into the church, for the respite, for the Grace.

Then, over one of those lovely medieval bridges, and a stop at a café .. with an adorable puppy who must must play with the boys. Five minutes out of the deluge. What a blessing! Onward again. We come upon a lovely old cross, the Crucero do Melide, 14th century, supposedly the oldest in Galicia.

As we come to Melide, the church bells are ringing! This has happened so many times on the Way, and I keep meaning to mention it, that they are so often ringing when we come into the village or town we are going to be staying in, no matter what time it is. Curious, and, glorious! We continue .. slogging along the main street. Oh, the loveliest fruit and vegetable shop! Such vivid colours in contrast to the pouring rain! We cross the street after a lady tells us not to wait for the signal, "It's broken." Now which way? An old man leans out of a window two stories up and gestures, yelling, "Albergue!" *Gracias Santiago por su ayuda!* We follow his pointing arm up a road, following the yellow Camino signs. Feet icy, soaking wet. Cold cold miserable. Then right and right again, arriving at a long line for the albergue. No way! This cold, this wet, we need a pensione. Not 50 steps onward, a hotel! Delicious salads while they prepare our room. A moment of upset when we find only a skylight in the bedroom .. but there is a bathroom, a bathtub(!) and it is warm and dry. We are so relieved, so grateful. T has a powerful realization. (Private.) Hugely important!

Out to the mercado. Then to visit the churches .. Sancti Spiritus, and, the Chapel of San Roque-San Pedro, which is full of locals. From the 1300s to the 1800s there was a hospice of Sancti Spiritus here where pilgrims on the Camino Primitivo joined the Camino Francès. The Roman road Via Traiana crossed through here. This area has been inhabited for more than 4000 years! Back to the hotel. Game shows, so fun! Hot showers. Delicious dinner. We are warm and safe! *Gracias Santiago!!*

Is the god the source, or is the god
the human manner of conceiving
of the force and energy
that supports the world?
In our tradition God is a male.
This male and female differentiation is made,
however,
within the field of time and space,
the field of duality.
If God is beyond duality,
You cannot say that God is a 'He".
You cannot say that God is a "She".
You cannot say that God is an "It."

Joseph Campbell

MELIDE TO ARZÚA

We slept until 7:30. Slow morning. Our desayuno is our provisions from the mercado last night .. biscuits and plain Griego yoghurt. Delicious. Pack up and head downstairs for colacao and café con leche. Then out, remembering where the Camino is, around the corner. To be sure, we ask at a bakery, and get croissants too. Yes, as we thought, thattaway. Stop to photograph the tiniest darlingest car ever. Then uphill, a church on the left, closed. Santa Maria de Melide, we think. Views over rooftops. Thank you Santiago for the overcast morning! We are all feeling so strong and good this morning as we walk. An old man, next to his grazing brown and white cow, one hand on its shoulder, one hand on his cane .. gazes into some other distance. A sheep comes toward the boys to say hello. I realize all of the roofs are ceramic instead of slate .. where did it change? Yesterday? Before Melide? Our companion plants today, eucalyptus, pine, hollyhock, and fern.

We come to Boente, the Iglesia de Santiago. Candles lit. Donativo for prayer cards. My heart feels such a sweet pain in these churches. *Love Peace .. Love Peace ..*

An elder wishes us "Buen viaje". A lovely smile exchanged between myself and another pilgrim. A conversation in French and English with a man about taking photos. He speaks about the law and his rights. I speak about good manners and integrity and the Camino and Grace. Silence. There is nothing else to be said, so he leaves. The boys and I pay attention to symbols. We continue onward, then pause while they give a lonely horse clumps of grass, which makes it happy. We talk about our favourite moments of the whole Camino.

We come to Castañeda, where the small amounts of lime .. that pilgrims carried from Triacastela centuries ago .. were put into lime kilns for building the cathedral in Santiago! I call to confirm our reservation (made by the cook at the albergue two days ago who was worried we, the boys especially, wouldn't have a place to stay without a reservation.) We feel good about this reservation, that sweet lady. It is a comfort because we are going along so slowly. We finally finally come to a bar, at 15:00, in Ribadiso, that we like. We are so hungry and tired. Yummy bocadillos and coffee and scrumptious fresh orange juice.

Only 40 kilometres to go to Santiago! It rains. *No problema*, as it's the first time all day. Restored, the boys full of ideas, happily talking, we walk down into the valley, across the medieval bridge over the River Iso, stop at the albergue for a sello for our credencials. Walking, both M and T have profound awarenesses! They are illuminated like candles in the rain.

Finally, we come to the gas station outside Arzúa. Per direction, I call the pensione people. He comes to pick us up. Whisked away a kilometre off the Way. The pensione lady is so sweet. Crackers for dinner, sadly, because it's pouring and we are who knows where. A bit of television, and hot showers. Comfy clean beds. I ask the proprietor to explain where we are. I do not want to feel out of touch with the Camino. Here, we are 37 kilometres from Santiago. It is only because it is night that I do not understand, she says. She is such a dear soul! Bless the *calefacción*, the heating, here! *Gracias Santiago por todos!*

Seek on high bare trails
Sky reflecting violets
Mountain-top jewels

Matsuo Basho

Arzúa to Santa Irene

Awoke to torrential rain and stong winds. Ah well, we repaired our flimsy ponchos last night after yesterday's bout with the elements. Blessed duct tape! We are wearing raincoats and rain pants. We have pack covers, and, with the ponchos, maybe we'll be dry! Out into it. Grateful to stop for desayuno. The proprietor deals with the crowd with a constant flurry of pastries and café con leches and zumo naranja natural (so many fabulous machines we've seen .. some with roller coaster tracks for the oranges to roll along) .. The floor is soaking wet, the peregrinos are soaking wet. It takes many coffees and cigarettes for some to get the nerve to go back out into the rain. Two café con leches for me .. onward! *Ultreia!*

The interesting thing about walking in the rain is that we really cannot see anything except the next few steps. From time to time we are overtaken by other pilgrims, and cyclists. Too few of the latter have bells and it's an awful shock as they whoosh up behind those who are walking; inside the noisy raincoats and ponchos, one never hears them coming. We are walking through woodland .. the lovely pungence of eucalyptus, sometimes pine also, and, the Galician constant of cow manure. We glimpse hollyhocks and ferns. Rocks everywhere. Three huge boulders which the boys promptly climb atop. Many different green mosses. Broken branches from the high winds. A fallen tree with holly that we squeeze past. Streams flooding their banks. Long stretches of mud. Inevitably, we all end up with water and mud in our shoes .. waterlogged.

At some point, we come out into a clearing with a single building, a café. Fogged windows. Open the door. The place is packed to the rafters with peregrinos and backpacks. It makes me laugh. Everything, everyone, is soggy. Even the perpetual café-bar cigarette smoke cannot rise due to the humidity in the room. People almost coming to blows over chairs. We find two barstools for the boys. *Thank you Santiago!* Colacao and coffee and sellos for our credenciales. A German fellow offers the boys some of his chocolate, and, when we leave, the café owner smilingly gives each boy a small chocolate bar!

Outside, Santiago holds off the rain long enough for me to take a photo and for us to get our ponchos on. So I'll have one photo from this day. It's horizontal rain and wind continuing for hours more. We are soggy .. beyond soggy, ponchos notwithstanding. We each have to find that place of tolerance and detachment. Then, beyond that, to blessing .. the Way, the rain, the world .. *Peace Love .. always ..*

Out of grey sheets of rain, another bar. How far to Santa Irene? One kilometre! Hallelujah! By road or by path? As we look at both choices, the angels (from the day enroute to Hontanas) appear! What a miracle to see their sweet faces! She says she was just thinking of us a few minutes ago, which makes us all smile. They are taking the path and continuing to Santiago de Compostela today. We take the road, pause to be sure .. and here comes a group of peregrinos led by an Irish fellow. He assures us the road is faster and drier than the path. Fortunately, most of the oncoming traffic veers toward the center of the road! A few minutes of walking and there! On the left, our (private) albergue. Thank God! The proprietor opens the door. It's warm, dry, charming. An old house. Sleeps fifteen. The other peregrinos are a loud, laughing bunch of Spaniards, ecstatic about walking to Santiago tomorrow. For us, it will be the day after. Later, I am lamenting the rain, and a lady laughs and says it will be hot and sunny this weekend in Santiago, didn't I know?! Oh, what a wonderful wonderful idea! *O Santiago, gracias por su amabilidad ..*

We become what we love
and, who we love
shapes what we become.
If we love things, we become a thing.
If we love nothing, we become nothing.
Imitation is not a literal mimicking of Christ,
rather it means becoming the image of the beloved,
an image disclosed though transformation.
This means we are to become
vessels of God's compassionate love for others.

Santa Clara of Assisi

Santa Irene to
Santiago de Compostela

We woke up this morning. As T said, "blessed sleep, blessed desayuno, blessed albergue" and .. we just kept on walking! We are here a day earlier than we planned .. without stopping for lunch. 12 hours after we left Santa Irene, now at 21:36, WE ARE HERE! In the heart of Santiago de Compostela, beyond exhausted, but we could not stop walking!

We paused at the hermitage of San Marcos del Monte del Gozo to take a deep breath. We paused at the outskirts of Santiago, at a hostel .. but we felt ourselves so close, so close .. we had to continue. Coming into the narrow winding streets of the ancient part of Santiago, of such a huge city, was shocking somehow, the finality of each step perhaps.

The dear Camino brought us to the cathedral .. gently, gently. We offered our initial thanks to Santiago. Further, the boys touched brows with the statue of Maestro Mateo, then touched the Tree of Jesse. Now we are at our hotel, replete with many feelings. Our view is of the Cathedral .. *O Santiago, gracias por su Camino .. O Santiago ..*

Tenets of the Heart
1. Accept myself
2. Accept others

SANTIAGO DE COMPOSTELA

We slept in. Such a luxury. We have desayuno at 11:00 at a gorgeous café on the plaza of two levels. Then we go into the cathedral for the Pilgrims Mass. We are seated in the second row on the transept. More and more pilgrims, and tourists, crowd into the cathedral, until it seems it must be overflowing out the doors. A nun glides into the centre, in front of the altar, and begins to sing so exquisitely. Her voice, the notes soaring up and up and up. The service is beautiful, formal, a benediction. We are sitting next to an older sweet prayerful pilgrim couple .. she translates the Latin for me.

Suddenly, midway through the mass, two rude men push past standing pilgrims and try to shove the boys and crowd into our pew, and are met by my protective "No!" as I am overcome by an intense resonating voice, the same voice I heard in San Juan de Ortega, but much louder: *"Esta es la casa de Dios! This is God's house!"* Amazingly, the two quickly turn and skulk away. I am stunned by this. The resonance continues like huge waves inside me. Then slowly I am filled with silence, and then .. with peace. Deep abiding peace.

Communion. The sweet couple beside me share the communion wafer he received for them. The beauty of their faces makes me weep. Oh look! Much to the delight of the entire cathedral, eight red-robed *tiraboleiros* bring in the huge huge silver *botafumeiro*, attaching it to a strong rope with sailors' knots, then lighting it. As the tiraboleiros pull in concert, the botafumeiro leaps up and swings in huge arcs above the pews of the transepts .. clouds of Grace and favours, of the holy healing scent, fill the cathedral. Prayers .. *O Santiago .. estamos aqui .. estamos aqui! Gracias, siempre gracias Santiago!* I am touched so deeply with awe. The sweet lady next to me tells me the botafumeiro is not brought out very often anymore. Thus today's is a great blessing for all. Ah, *Gracias Santiago por su amabilidad!* I am so grateful to have shared a pew today with such beautiful sweet pilgrims. After the service, the crowd disperses. We wait a bit, breathing in the mystery. Then we prosaically purchase pilgrim's shells from the church shop, and I find some postcards. Indeed, as He said earlier, it is written on one of the postcards: *Seas bienvenido a mi casa*. The bienvenidos part, not so much for those two rude people, but the casa, yes, yes it is His.

The boys and I go to the Parador Dos Reis Católicos for the most luxurious delicious lunch imaginable. We savour every moment, for two hours! As we step out onto the plaza, the cathedral calls to me, to us .. the pilgrim steps which we began last night, and continued this morning, still must be completed. We stand in line to hug Santiago. I have my list in my hand .. *O Santiago please bless all of these people, please set them free. Please bless this world with peace. Please hear the prayers of all whom I have carried to you.* As I touch the mantle of His statue .. *I am flooded by a pouring Light of sparking radiance ..* Overcome, I fall to my knees, raised by the attending priest .. he has me touch it again, and *it is now a vast waterfall of pouring radiant Light .. so intense .. so much Love .. so much ..* I cry out and the priest pulls me to one side so the line can continue while I sob and sob and he tries to tell me in Spanish what .. in the world, in eternity .. has just happened. Words, language, time, comprehension are all beyond me. My beloved boys tell me later that each has their own moments with Santiago, coming through the line again until I am finally able to walk down the stairs with them. *O Santiago!*

I put my sunglasses on. We go down to the crypt, to leave the list there, and the walnuts of the sweet lady of Lorca. We send blessings and thanks to all who helped us on our Way. Then we go up and sit on a pew, the boys patiently waiting with me, as I am still held in the enormity of the unspoken, the beyond spoken within me .. I weep, breathe, pray .. offering my gratitude over and over and over again ..

After some unknown span of time, we come down from the mountain .. and go find the compostela office. The line is long, a slow procession up the wide worn stone steps, inside, up and up, turning slowly. There is so much to contemplate. Our long journey. The boys and I look at our credenciales .. so many sellos .. so many places .. so much have we experienced .. so many prayers .. so many blessings. The room with the long table with many seated functionaries. The ritual questions asked and answered. Our credenciales stamped. Our *compostelas* filled in by hand, rolled into a tube. Done. Oh no .. we are done! Can we be? Now what?! I feel breathless, then breathe, smiling, realizing we have only to contemplate, to pray, to listen in stillness, and we will be given direction. *Gracias Dios .. Gracias Maria .. O Gracias Santiago .. por todos .. siempre .. en la eternidad ..*

May you be blessed.
May you be well.
May you be illuminated
by the Camino de Santiago.

9 780995 510364